Contributions to Islamic Studies:
Iran, Afghanistan
and Pakistan

THE DANISH RESEARCH COUNCIL FOR THE HUMANITIES
Distributed by
AARHUS UNIVERSITY PRESS

Initiativområdet Islam i Nutiden
Publikation nr. 3

Research Programme on Contemporary Islam
Publication no. 3

Edited by Christel Braae and Klaus Ferdinand

Distributed by
AARHUS UNIVERSITY PRESS
Aarhus University
DK-8000 Aarhus C
Denmark

CONTENTS

PREFACE

In 1982 the Danish Research Council for the Humanities initiated the research programme "Comtemporary Islamic Studies",
the objective of which was to promote and develop research,
particularly into modern religious trends and development in
the Muslim World.

The background to this research programme wasthe apparent
growth of importance of Islam, politically and socially, in
the Middle East and in other Muslim areas, as well as in Denmark, where Muslims since the 1970's have formed the second
largest religious community.

The research programme has so far concentrated on the 19th
and the 20th century, a period characterised by confrontations between the Muslim and the expanding imperialist Western powers.

A number of researchers have been employed under the programme, and several seminars and workshops have taken place with
the participation of guest lecturers.

In 1982, the research programme commenced the project "Islam,
State and Society" focusing on Iran, Afghanistan and Pakistan. It was completed with an international conference, the
papers of which are present in print.[1] In 1983 a project
on "Islamic Groups in Soviet Central Asia" followed.[2]

Since 1985 the research programme has focussed on Muslim
communities in Denmark, and various topics are being cove-
red.

The present volume presents part of the work of an inter-
disciplinary research group on "Islam, State and Society".
The contribution by mag. scient. Jan Ovesen is not included
here, as it has been printed elsewhere.[3] Prior commitments
prevented mag. scient. Asger Christensen from contributing
in writing, although he actively participated in the research
group. Finally, Dr. Mehdi Mozaffari's valuable contribution
could not be contained within an article. It is at present
being published as a seperate book.[4]
The contributions in this volume deal with the historical
development of Iran (Peter Christensen: The Qajar State),
Afghanistan (Asta Olesen: The Political Role of Islam in
Afghanistan During the Reign of Amir Abdur Rahman Khan (1880-
1901), and Pakistan (Frede Højgaard: Islam and Pakistan).

With their different perspectives these contributions high-
light the distinctive role of Islam in the recent developments of these countries.

I would like to thank all the members of the research group
on "Islam, State and Society", and, in particular, the three
contributors to this volume.

                                    Klaus Ferdinand

NOTES:

1)   Klaus Ferdinand & Mehdi Mozaffari (Eds.): ISLAM: State
      and Society. Studies on Asian Topics (Scandinavian In-
      stitute of Asian Studies), No. 12, London (Curzon
      Press Ldt.) 1987.

2)   The researcher is cand. mag. & mag art. Ewa Chylinski
      with the following publications:
      Sovjettisk uddannelsespolitik og muslimer i Central-
      asien. In: Nordic Journal of Soviet and East European
      Studies, Vol. 1 No. 1, 1984: 43 - 65.
      Islam in Central Asia. In Ewa Chylinski (Ed.): Soviet
      Central Asia: Continuity and Change. Esbjerg 1985:
      56 - 60.
      Social and Cultural Anthropology on Soviet Central
      Asia: A Western European Perspective. (forthcoming
      Utrecht).
      Supranational and Subnational. Symbols and Rituals in
      Soviet Central Asia. Forthcoming in: Nordic Journal of
      Soviet and East European Studies.

3)   Jan Ovesen: The Construction of Ethnic Identities; the
      Nuristani and the Pashai. In: A. Jacobson-Widding
      (Ed.): Identity: Personal and Socio-Cultural. A Sympo-
      sium. Uppsala 1983, and Jan Ovesen: On the Cultural
      Heritage of the Pashai. In: Anthropos Vol- 79, 1984:
      384 - 407.

4)   Mehdi Mozaffari: ISLAM: Models of Power. From Muhammad
      to Khomaini. New York (M.E. Sharpe Inc.) 1987.

THE QAJAR STATE

by

Peter Christensen

The desire to understand the background of the 1978-79 revolution has in several respects led to revisions of the view of recent Iranian history current until now. Previous discussion has understandably been focused on the development of *shii* ideology and the position of the *ulama*. The frequent claim that *shia* Islam as a matter of principle considers the secular state illegitimate, and that a constant tension has therefore existed for centuries between *ulama* and state (e.g. Algar 1969 and 1972), has been criticized; and it has been convincingly argued that the *ulama*'s claim to a doctrinally based special relationship with the state was first clearly formulated in the 1960's (Eliash 1979; Floor 1980. The practice of the *ulama* under both the Safavids and the Qajars indicated moreover that as a rule they accepted and contributed to the legitimation (and thus to the maintenance) of the secular state.

The participation of the *ulama* in opposition to the state during the period around the turn of the century, and again in the 1960's and 70's, cannot thus be adequately explained in terms of *shii* doctrine, but must be seen in the context of the specific historical conditions prevailing in each individual case.

Any analysis of the background of the political conflicts around the turn of the century - first and foremost the Tobacco Protest of 1891-92 and the Constitutional Revolution of 1905-06 - must in my opinion also involve a revision of our view of the "traditional" state. Most studies of the history of Iran in the 19th and 20th centuries take it for granted that the Qajar state was particularly inefficient and corrupt and thus an impotent plaything of the

great imperialist powers. In this article a contrary hypothesis will be argued: that the Qajar state should be seen
as a dynamic factor whose significance has been obscured by
the great changes which took place afterwards in Iranian
society under Pahlavi rule. As support for this hypothesis
I will emphasize, among other things, phenomena and developments which, because of the preconceived, ethnocentric picture we have of 19th-century Iran, have not quite achieved
the status of "historical facts about the Qajar state";
that is, which do not form a part of the pool of, so to
speak, "canonized" data on the subject. The following account thus consists both of narrative and discursive elements.

The Qajars were the heirs to an empire which traditionally stretched from the Oxus and the Hindu Kush in the
east to the Mesopotamian river basin in the west. It was
the power and authority of the empire which bound this extensive area together; it did not form a geographical and
economic unit. On the contrary, mountains and deserts
split it up into a number of regions which were self-sufficient in all essentials. Politically, the regional divisions were reflected in the existence of numerous local
rulers who acknowledged, more of less willingly, the
supremacy of the empire, but who otherwise enjoyed a considerable degree of autonomy. The constant tension between local powers and the empire constituted in my opinion
an important dynamic variable in the history of Iran.

Among the local rulers the tribal leaders or *khans*
enjoyed a special position by virtue of their control of
the military potential of the nomads.[1] Nomadic society
produced on its own initiative and without expense to the
state horses and well-trained cavalrymen, and as long as
cavalry reigned supreme on the battlefield - and was the
only armed force mobile enough to keep a far-flung empire
united - the nomads constituted a unique resource. Since

the 11th century all Iranian empires had been built up by
leaders who had been capable of mobilizing the nomads. The
constantly recurring problem for these leaders was keeping
the warriors in check as soon as the phase of actual conquest with its opportunities for plundering and social ad-
vancement, was over, and preventing the rise of rival empire-
builders.

One way of solving this problem was to pursue a policy
of expansion and to lead the nomad warriors on large-scale
plundering campaigns against surrounding societies. Examples
of this were the campaign of the Safavids against Georgie
and Nadir Shah's attack on India and sack of Delhi in 1739.

A more permanent solution consisted of attaching some
of the *khans* to the empire. Tribal organization as a rule
granted quite limited powers to the *khans*. The empire, on
the other hand, could grant some of them wealth and status
by appointing them to office (for example as governors) and
by allocating to them incomes from agriculture in the form
of *tuyul*.[2] The *khans* who were given this sort of preferen-
tial treatment could then by redistributing their new wealth
increase their power within the tribe and eliminate rival
leaders. At the same time they had to maintain good relations with their benefactor, the empire, which they did
primarily by acknowledging the supremacy of the *Shah* and
paying some form of tribute. The disadvantage of this
system, seen from the empire's point of view, was that the
more powerful of the *khans*, by combining the military might
of their tribes with the fiscal resources of a region,
achieved a considerable degree of genuine autonomy (Woods
1976; Reid 1978; Minorsky 1943, p. 14 ff; Röhrborn 1966;
Savory 1964, pp. 114-128; Hinz 1933, pp. 19-100). Both the
Aq Qoyunlu and the early Safavid empires were thus distinct-
ly decentralized in character.[3]

The third and most radical solution, which consisted
of reducing the importance of, or completely eliminating
the nomads as a military factor, presented itself as a
possibility when the battles of Bashkent (1473) and Chaldiran

(1514) demonstrated the superior strength of artillery and
musket-bearing infantry over the nomad cavalry.[4] Building
up an alternative military force consisting of musket-bearing infantry on the Ottoman model was the central element
in the attempts of Abbas I (1587-1629) and Safi I (1629-42)
to quell the power of the *Qizilbash* leaders (Minorsky 1943,
p. 30 ff.; Banani 1978; Lockhart 1959, pp. 89-98). At the
same time Abbas I made use of more traditional ploys. For
example, he tried to sow strife between the *khans* by showing
favouritism towards tribes outside the *Qizilbash* confederation; he enticed rank-and-file tribesmen with the prospect
of participation in plundering campaigns against Georgia,
and he attempted to jockey the *Qizilbash* leaders out of the
imperial administration by appointing his Georgian and
Armenian slaves as governors (and in a few cases even as
khans). (On Safavid administrative policy see Minorsky 1943;
Banani 1978; Röhrborn 1966). It was true that they tended,
like other governors, to establish local roots and make the
offices hereditary, but they disposed far less than the
tribal *khans* over their own military resources and were thus
easier to remove again.[5]

Yet the Safavid attempt at centralization was a failure,
first and foremost because the alternative military apparatus
which Abbas I had built up was too costly in the long run,
and had to be cut back. After Abbas II (1642-67) the tribal
khans and other local rulers increasingly regained their
autonomy.

The last residue of Safavid power was broken by the
revolts of the Afghan Ghilzay and Abdali tribes and the fall
of Isfahan (1722), and after this there followed several attempts to build up a new empire. The Afghans proved in-
capable of consolidating their conquests and were defeated
within a few years by Nadir Shah. The latter did not belong
to the group of *khans*; it would be more accurate to describe
him as a warlord who, by virtue of his military and political talents and a charismatic personality, was able to

mobilize support, first and foremost from the great Turkish
and Afghan tribes in Eastern Iran. With his ceaseless cam-
paigning he reestablished a unified political authority over
the whole Iranian area and took steps towards a revival of
the administrative and economic base of the empire. But the
army was held together solely by his personal authority (and
the prospects of plunder), and the embryonic basis of his
empire therefore dissolved with his death in 1947.

One of his generals, Ahmad Shah Durrani, whose military
power base was the Abdali tribe in the Qandahar region, then
created an Afghan "mini-empire" which was mainly held together by means of continual looting in the Panjab and
Kashmir. Ahmad Shah and his successor Timur Shah (+1793)
also enjoyed a formal supremacy over the *khans* and warlords
in Khurasan, Sistan and Baluchistan (Kinneir 1813, p. 170;
Malcolm 1829 II, P. 235 f; Fasa'i 1972, p. 92 f.), but an
attempt to extend this sovereignty farther west had been
thwarted already in 1755 by the Turkish Qajar tribe in
Gurgan-Mazandaran, whose leaders themselves had ambitions
of seizing imperial power.

The realization of these ambitions was prevented in the
first instance by a rival warlord, Karim Khan Zand, who had
succeeded, in the course of the 1750's, in mobilizing the
tribes in South Western Iran and gaining control of Fars
and Iraq-e Ajam. Later he extended his sovereignty to
Azarbayjan and Khuzistan. By playing on internal tribal
conflicts he was able in 1758 to isolate and defeat Muhammad
Hasan Khan, the most ambitious of the Qajar *khans* (Dunbuli
1833, p. 6 f.).

Karim Khan's command of Southern and Central Iran was
based not only on the tribal warriors, but also on cooperation with local leaders in the form of landowners, representatives of the *bazaris*, etc., and the failure of this cooperation was the reason for the collapse of Zand rule. (On the
career of Karim Khan-e Zand see Lambton (1977).

The death of Karim Khan in 1779 was the cue for pro-
tracted conflicts within his family. Rival princes each

mobilized armies of tribal warriors, and while they were
thus battling for power the local rulers in, among other
places, Yazd, Tabas, Laristan, Kirman and Khuzistan reas-
serted their independence. In the course of a few years
the Zand realm was reduced in territory to Fars and parts
of Iraq-e Ajam (Fasa'i 1972, p. 26 f.). At the same time
Aqa Muhammad, the son of Muhammad Hasan Khan, had established
himself as the leader of the Qajars. Having demonstrated his
political talents by settling the constant disputes between
the two clans of the tribe, the Qoyunlu and the Devehlu,[6]
and his military qualifications by beating off a Zand assault on Astarabad in 1784, he entered into the struggle for
empire. (For accounts of the struggle for power inside the
Qajar tribe see Fasa'i 1972, pp. 17, 74f, Dunbuli 1833,
p. 10 ff, Malcolm 1829 II, p. 205).

The outcome of the long-standing strife between Qajar
and Zand was settled when a number of local leaders in Fars
realized that it was no longer in their interest to be
caught up in the fate of the disunited Zand dynasty, and to
have their properties and clients exposed to looting and the
extortion of tribute by now one, now the other army. In 1791
the *kalantar* of Shiraz,[7] Hajji Ibrahim Khan, declared himself for Aqa Muhammad and closed the gates of the city against
the Zand leader Lutf Ali Khan.[8]

Hajji Ibrahim later explained his motives to the British
envoy Malcolm:

> "None (...) except some plundering soldiers,
> cared whether a zond or a Kujur was upon the
> throne; but all desired that Persia should be
> great and powerful, and enjoy internal tran-
> quility."
>
> (Malcolm 1829 II, p. 183)

The importance of Hajji Ibrahim's "treason" for the further
course of the war renders it necessary to comment briefly
on weaponry. Throughout the 18th century handguns had become increasingly widespread. "Muskets, pistols and cara-
bins, are made and mounted in most of the great towns,"
observed Kinneir at the beginning of the 19th century

(Kinneir 1813, pp. 36 f, 83, 198; Waring 1807, p. 32;
Ouseley 1819 II, p. 58), and a *tufang* (musket) seems to have
cost much less than a good horse (cf. Inalcik 1975, pp. 195-
217). Learning to use it was reasonably easy - while on the
other hand it took years to train even a tolerably competent
cavalryman. Anyone, in short, could invest in a musket and
take service with the highest bidder.[9] These *tufangchis*
did not have the mobility of the nomad cavalry, but their
firepower turned out to be increasingly decisive in pitched
battles and sieges. With their appearance the nomad monopoly of military power really began to crumble.[10]

Both Aqa Muhammad and his opponents enlisted several
thousand *tufangchis* for their armies. Since the *tufangchis*
were mercenaries, their loyalty was in the first instance to
those who paid for their services. A large number of
tufangchis in the Zand army were paid by Hajji Ibrahim and
led by his brothers (Fasa'i 1972, p. 42 ff; Malcolm 1829 II,
p. 182), and when he changed sides Lutf Ali Khan lost not
only access to the economic resources of Shiraz, but also
the majority of his musketeers. He could still gather
Kurdish and Lur tribal warriors, but this was not enough to
defend Fars against the Qajars. He therefore had to fall
back on Kirman, where he was finally defeated in 1794 and
executed shortly afterwards.

The victory over the Zands had in reality only given
Aqa Muhammad mastery of the settlements along the edge of
the central deserts. The rest of Iran was divided among rulers who acknowledged his supremacy only grudgingly, or not
at all. In the east the rulers preferred purely formal recognition of Durrani sovereignty.[11] Aqa Muhammad, who saw
himself as the heir of the Safavids and took every opportunity to underscore that his exercise of power was in accordance with historical tradition, had up to now refused to be
crowned as Shah, giving as his grounds that "as long as the
whole population of Persia does not obey my rule, it is not
becoming that I call myself king" (Fasa'i 1972, p. 67;

Malcolm 1829 II, p. 287). It was now the turn of the refractory local rulers to feel his might. In 1795 he attacked Northern Azarbayjan, defeated the Javanshir tribe
and demanded - referring to the above-mentioned historical
tradition - the submission of the Prince of Georgia:

> "Shah Esma'il Safavi ruled over the province
> of Georgia (...) As most of the provinces of
> Persia have come into our possession now, you
> must, according to ancient law, consider Geor-
> gia part of the empire and appear before our
> majesty. You have to confirm your obedience;
> then you may remain in the possession of your
> governorship. If you do not do this, you will
> be treated as the others."
>
> (Fasa'i 1972, p. 66)

When the Prince, confident of Russian protection, refused,
Aqa Muhammad invaded and ravaged the country just as his
Safavid predecessors had done.

Following this victory Aqa Muhammad was able to have
himself crowned Shah in Tehran (1796). The ceremony was
carried out on Safavid lines, again to emphasize historical
continuity (Fasa'i 1972, p. 68). The same year he began
the offensive against the rulers in Khurasan. Mashad ca-
pitulated quickly, but then the campaign had to be broken
off, as a report came that Russian forces had attacked
Azarbayjan. The following spring, just as he was about to
start a counter-attact north of the Araks, Aqa Muhammad was
assassinated.[12]

The empire of Nadir Shah had not survived its creator,
and the Zand state had been fragmented by the civil wars
after the death of Karim Khan; if the Qajar state did not
share their fate, this was due to the efforts Aqa Muhammad
had made to secure a broad political base for it. It is
true that the army broke up on the news of his death: the
tribal warriors went home or rallied round those Qoyunlu
princes who were impatient to seize power. But both the
governor of Tehran (who belonged to the Devehlu tribe) and
the Grand Vizier Hajji Ibrahim, who controlled the troops
from Fars and the *Mazandarani tufangchi*s loyally supported
the heir designate, Fath Ali, who could therefore subdue

his rivals with no great difficulty (Fasa'i 1972, pp. 75 f, 85). It was also an indication of the stability of the new state that subjugated rulers and *khans* remained passive on the whole. It was only in Azarbayjan and Khurasan that the tribes made an attempt to regain their independence (Dunbuli 1833, pp. 29 ff, 49 ff).

The most important task ahead of Fath Ali Shah was the completion of the reconquest of the areas which belonged historically to the empire, above all Khurasan, where the local warlords were most stubborn in their refusal to re-cognize Qajar supremacy (Fasa'i 1972, pp. 93, 103 ff, 155 f, 164 f). Nishapur was taken in 1799, Mashhad surrendered in 1803 (and the local ruler was executed to set an example), but after this the Qajars had to break off the offensive and concentrate on the defence of Transcaucasia, which had been invaded by Russia in 1804.

The first year's fighting proved that the army with which Aqa Muhammad had won his empire could perhaps create difficulties for, but could not prevent the Russian advance. The explanation for this is hardly to be found in the supe-riority of the Russian Weaponry, as at the beginning of the 19th century there was still no conclusive difference in this respect between European and Oriental armies. Even during the Afghan War of 1838-42 the bayonet was in fact still the British infantry's most important weapon. The European superiority originated in better organization, discipline and understanding of tactics (cf. Dunbuli 1833, pp. 239, 347 f, 396 f), and in more plentiful economic re-sources which permitted the maintenance of standing armies. The Qajars were left with the problem of waging a defensive war with an army which in the first place was used to being rewarded with booty in conquered areas and in the second place could only be deployed at full strength in the summer half of the year. In October at the latest the nomad caval-ry had to be sent home, as there was no longer pasture for the horses (Dunbuli 1833, pp. 293, 352); apart from a few

scattered *tufangchi* garrisons the country lay wide open for
the Russians in the winter (Dunbuli 1833, pp. 235, 254;
Fasa'i 1972, p. 119).

The leader of the Qajar defence, Crown Prince Abbas
Mirza, began therefore in 1806-7 to build up a standing
infantry force organized and armed on European lines
(Dunbuli 1833, p. 306 ff; Fasa'i 1972, p. 122). This
nizam-e jadid (i.e. "new army") was recruited among the
Azarbayjanis and the former *tufangchi*s and trained by French,
and later British advisers.[13] In the short run the reform
meant a weakening of the Iranian defence of Transcaucasia.
The nomad cavalry could not perhaps beat the Russians in
open battle, but because of their mobility they were a constant threat to the Russian supply lines (and had thus been
able to force General Zizianov to raise the siege of Erivan
in 1804)(Dunbuli 1833, pp. 204 f, 208 f; Fasa'i 1972, p. 109).
The *nizam-e jadid* was, however, intended as an army which
could wage war on European terms and meet the enemy in open
battle. This happened at Azlanduz in 1812. Abbas Mirza
suffered a serious defeat, and on the conclusion of peace
the following year the Qajar state had to cede Georgia,
Shirvan and Qarabagh. An attempt to reconquer these provinces in 1826-28 ended in new defeats and the loss of the
last territory north of the River Araks.

In spite of these setbacks the Qajars carried out fairly thoroughly the military reorganization begun by Abbas
Mirza. Recruitment - which had originally been confined to
Azarbayjan - was extended and systematized (Fasa'i 1972, p.
221 f); a "polytechnic school" *(Daru'l-Funun)* was founded
in order, among other things, to train officers, and European advisers were constantly called in. According to Iranian
surveys the army in the 1870's had reached an effective
strength of between 40,000 and 60,000 men (Sheikholeslami
1978, p. 210).

European observers agreed almost without exception in
describing the new army in very negative terms. The pointed
out that the soldiers were undisciplined and almost unpaid,

the officers corrupt and incompetent, etc., and British observers, who feared a Russian drive through Iran, complained
that the Qajars, in Curzon's words, had cut "the locks of
the Persian Samson" by weakening the tribes and the irregular nomad cavalry (Curzon 1892 II, p. 594 f (also vol. I
chap. xvii)).

But the military reforms must not be evaluated purely
on the basis of the *nizam-e jadid*'s capacity to withstand
European armies. The British military adviser Justin Sheil
commented after many years' work in Iran that

> "no irregular troops, whether they be native
> Persians or Koords, Arabs, Afghans, Toorkomans,
> or Turks, are able to contend with the dis-
> ciplined Persian forces."
>
> (Sheil 1856, p. 381)

- and he was certainly not blind to their weak sides. With
the formation of the *nizam-e jadid* the process which the
advent of the *tufangchi*s had ushered in was complete: the
state had made itself almost independent of the military
potential of the nomads, and had acquired a force which,
despite all its obvious weaknesses and shortcomings, was
effective enough to subdue all the local rulers.

This did not mean that the Qajars thenceforth always
chose military solutions to disputes. Like their predecessors they attempted to establish ties with local potentates
by means of favours, marriage alliances, hostages etc.
(Fraser 1840 I, pp. 101 f, 111 f, II, p. 187; cf. Lambton,
"Ilat" in EI/2), but thanks to the *nizam-e jadid* they could
back up their demands with military force as a last resort.
Even if the tribes continued to prove refractory and in-
dulged at intervals in feuds, plundering and the refusal of
tribute, the difference from before was that no *khan*, however powerful, could any longer entertain realistic hopes
of seizing the throne from the dynasty in power.[14] The
nizam-e jadid changed the existing power structure in society, and it is indicative of the extent of the innovation
that it was in reality not a non-Muslim innovation at all,
but on the contrary a return to ancient Muslim principles.

The effective "Frankish" tactics, they asserted, had been
invented and recommended by the Prophet himself, but had
then later been forgotten by the Muslims (Dunbuli 1833, p.
306 ff).

After the wars with Russia the Qajar state again undertook the subjugation of rebellious potentates. In the second half of the 1830's Manuchih Khan Mutamidu'd-Davleh thus
initiated a number of hard-hitting drives against the *khans*
in Khuzistan (Layard 1846, pp. 31-36). Qajar control of the
province was extended step by step throughout the century
until only the *shaykh* of Muhammareh was left. However, he
managed to survive as a semi-autonomous ruler because Great
Britain, in accordance with its general policy in the Gulf,
held a protecting hand over him.

Great power intervention also checked the Qajar reconquest of Khurasan. Here the surviving warlords had attempted to exploit the 1826-28 war to liberate themselves,
and in response Abbas Mirza began an offensive against them
in 1830-31 during which the artillery of the new army played
a decisive role. Turshiz was taken, the mighty Zafaranlu
khan was defeated and forced into submission, and in 1833
Sarakhs, which had fallen into the hands of the Turcomans
of Marv, was stormed and the garrison massacred as a warning
that the Qajar state would no longer tolerate resistance in
an area it regarded as its territory (Watson 1866, p. 257 f).

After the deaths of Abbas Mirza and Fath Ali Shah,
Muhammad Shah (1834-48) took the next step and began to lay
siege to Herat, which was still in the hands of the Durrani
family. Expecting a quick Qajar victory, the Afghan rulers
of Qandahar found it wisest to recognize the supremacy of
the Shah (Norris 1967, p. 128). But the victory did not
materialize. Heavy diplomatic pressure and military threats
from Great Britain, which regarded Herat as the key to one
of the important approaches to India and considered Muhammad
Shah to be the obedient tool of Russia, forced the Shah in
1838 to raise the siege. Fearing the growing power of Dust
Muhammad, the leaders of the city later declared themselves

willing to recognize Qajar sovereignty, and in 1856 a Qajar
force was able to enter the city. But this again brought a
sharp reaction from Great Britain. A naval expedition was
sent to the Gulf, Bushir and Muhammareh were occupied, and
in order to avoid a major war with the British the Qajars
had to abandon Herat, which fell a few years later into the
hands of Dust Muhammad (1863).[15]

The next target of the Qajars was Marv. After the dis-
solution of Nadir Shah's empire the oasis, which was inhabi-
ted by Turcoman tribes, was to all intents and purposes independent, although it occasionally recognized the supremacy
of either Bukhara or Khiva. The economy of the oasis was to
a great extent based on plunder and slave-trading. The
Turcomans made constant incursions into Qajar territory,
where they attacked caravans and raided villages, whose inhabitants were carried off and sold in the slave markets in
Khiva and Bukhara (on the other hand the Kurdish tribes
which had settled in the Kopet Dagh region and had functioned
as defenders of the border in Safavid times made attacks on
the Turcomans)(e.g. Macgregor 1879 II, p. 83 ff and
O'Donovan 1882 II, p. 34 ff). All travellers' accounts
from the 19th century tell of the fear of the Turcomans in
Eastern Iran. To put an end to this permanent state of war
and pre-empt the threatened Russian expansion in Central
Asia the Qajars sent the governor of Mashhad in 1860 with a
considerable force - allegedly thirty thousand strong -
against Marv. During the difficult march through the desert
the force was almost annihilated by the Turcomans. Trans-
port problems, incompetent leadership and the fact that
there had not been time to deploy the artillery seem to
have been the reason for the first (and only) major defeat
of units of the *nizam-e jadid* by irregular tribal cavalry
(Eastwick 1864 II, p. 216; Sheikholeslami 1978, p. 216).
However, it was more fear of Russia than of the Turcomans
that caused the Qajar state to give up the attempt to reconquer the oasis. Nasiru'd-Din Shah requested political
(and material) support from Great Britain for a new assault

(Thornton 1954 (I), p. 564), but when this was refused he had to accept, by the terms of the Akbal-Khurasan Convention with Russia (1881) the setting of the north eastern boundary of Iran at Kopet Dagh. In the following year Russian armies subdued the Transcaspian Turcomans and occupied Marv. With this move, the partition of Khurasan became a reality. The Qajars had only managed to reconquer the western part of the former Iranian area; the rest went to Russia, and - thanks to the British intervention in the struggle for Herat - to the new Afghani state.

British intervention in favour of Afghanistan likewise prevented a complete reconquest of Sistan. Since 1800 the area had been divided up between *de facto* autonomous Afghani and Baluchi *khans* (Kinneir 1813, p. 193; Malcolm 1829 II, p. 237 f; Goldsmid 1876, p. 300 ff). Both the Qajar state and the Afghani *amirs* claimed sovereignty. Dust Muhammad occupied Farah in 1856, and in about 1860 the *amir* of Qayin - an East Iranian local ruler who had managed to keep his position by maintaining close ties with the Qajars - began a gradual reconquest on behalf of the Shah (On the *amirs* of Qayin see Malcolm 1829 II, p. 224 f; Goldsmid 1876, p. 337; Macgregor 1879 I, p. 169; Stewart 1911, p. 327). By playing on internal disputes between the tribal leaders he succeeded within ten years in subjugating the country west of the River Hilmand to Iran, and consolidated his gains by building forts and villages, by bringing Iranian colonists in from Kuhistan and Khurasan, and by repairing and widening the dams over the Hilmand, so that more water was directed into areas under Iranian control (Goldsmid 1876, pp. 259, 267, 271 f, 287). Shir Ali, Dust Muhammad's successor, responded by requesting help from Great Britain, and through British arbitration a border was fixed in 1871-72 between the Qajar state and Afghanistan in Sistan. The settlement acknowledged the existing situation by granting the Qajar state the areas of greatest potential value at the Hilmand delta, but at the same time set a limit to any further Qajar expansion.

Finally British intervention also checked the Qajars'
advance further south into Baluchistan-Makran. After the
death of Nadir Shah a *khan*ate had arisen in Kalat in Eastern
Baluchistan, formally subject to the Durrani empire. The
khan of Kalat was unable to keep the *sardars* (i.e. tribal
leaders) in the area under effective control, and had no
control at all of those in the west, where they made regular
raids on the settlements in the whole of South Eastern Iran
(Goldsmid 1876, p. 244). In connection with the annexation
of Sind and the Punjab the British gained control in the
1840's of the *khan* of Kalat and in return helped him in his
struggle against the rebellious *sardars*. At the same time
the Qajars occupied the oasis of Bampur in Western
Baluchistan, and throughout the following decades this
functioned as the base for a slow but sure expansion (Fasa'i
1972, p. 271; Goldsmid 1876, pp. 30, 34, 56, 72, 75 f;
Curzon 1892 II, p. 253 ff). Ibrahim Khan - the govenor of
Bam-Narmashir from c. 1850-1884 - exhibited great energy
(and often just as great brutality) in his pacification of
the area up as far as Chah Bahar and Pishin. To contain
this advance and keep the *khan*ate of Kalat as a buffer between India and the Qajar state a British commission fixed
a border in 1870-71 which was an acknowledgement, as in
Sistan, of the Qajar conquests up to then,but which at the
same time prevented further expansion (Goldsmid 1876, pp.
xiv ff, 62; Sykes 1902, p. 104 ff).

The intervention of great powers was in short the
primary reason for the failure of the Qajars to realize
their ambitions of re-establishing the historically defined Iranian empire at its full extent.

Concurrently with the attempt to reconquer the lost
territories, the Qajars had, as already indicated, tight-
ened their grip on tribes and local rulers within the area
they controlled. Even though widespread instances of nomad
settlement took place, the Qajars - who after all had their
own roots in nomad society - were much more willing than
their successors to accept the existence of the nomadic way

of life; but they made consistent and successful efforts to
reduce the power of the *khans* in society. This they did
partly by playing rival tribes and *khans* off against one
another, partly by means of military force.[16] A number of
hard-liner governors, such as Manuchihr Khan (Khuzistan),
Ibrahim Khan (Baluchistan) and the two sons of Abbas Mirza,
Farhad Mirza (Fars) and Murad Mirza Hishamu's-Saltaneh
(Khurasan), gradually succeeded in subduing tribes and
eliminating the majority of the many local rulers and warlords (e.g. Fasa'i 1972, pp. 219, 223 ff, 244, 268 f, 336 f,
343 f, 386 ff, 416; Fraser 1840 II, p. 187 f). Local uprisings, tribal feuds and the like were on the whole reduced
to the status of minor disturbances of the peace which did
not pose any threat to state control. According to Sheil,
in the second half of the 19th century there were only three
tribes left which possessed real political power: the
Bakhtiyari (Iraq-e Ajam and Northern Khuzistan), the
Zafaranlu (Khurasan) and the Qashqa'i (Fars) (Sheil 1856,
p. 395). Among the local rulers only the *Shaykh* of
Muhammareh and the *Amir* of Qayin kept some degree of autonomy (the former could thank British protection for this,
while the latter based his position on loyal cooperation
with the Qajar state).

The general weakening of the power of the *khans* is apparent from the fact that the Qajars - unlike the Safavids
- succeeded in keeping them out of all the important governorships and the imperial central administration (Malcolm
1829 II, p. 436). Governorships were filled as a rule by
the Shah's male relatives - under due supervision by a
vazir - and by loyal soldiers and officials like Manuchihr
Khan. The leadership of the imperial bureaucracy - and
above all the office of Grand Vizier (from 1810 onwards
called the *sadr-e azam*) - was entrusted to members of the
rich patrician families who had often performed administrative duties for changing rulers for generations, and who
were in general opposed to the power of the *khans*.[17]

The career of Hajji Ibrahim can serve as an illustration of the status of these families and their relationship to the state. His family had amassed a considerable fortune by the end of the Safavid era - mainly through trade - and had invested part of it in public enterprises (the building of a mosque and a *madraseh*). Both because of this fortune and his prestige as a public benefactor Hajji Ibrahim's father had succeeded in having himself appointed *kadkhuda* ("vice-mayor") of several quarters in Shiraz. He was dismissed by Nadir Shah, but the family returned to grace again under the Zand dynasty, and Hajji Ibrahim was appointed *kalantar*. As mentioned above, he changed sides during the Zand-Qajar war and became Grand Vizier under Aqa Muhammad and Fath Ali Shah. His brothers and sons occupied a number of leading posts at the same time within the central and provincial administrations (Fasa'i 1972, p. 96 f; Malcolm 1829 II, p. 175 ff).

Hajji Ibrahim's fall from office and execution in 1801 may be seen as a concession to envious Qajar princes and those *khans* who were still powerful. It is also possible that the Shah himself had misgivings about the power of the family (according to Malcolm the wish to confiscate the huge fortune which the family had amassed in public service also played som part)(Malcolm 1828 II, p. 155). But in spite of Hajji Ibrahim's dramatic fate there was no fundamental change in Qajar policy, and the office of Grand Vizier and all other administrative posts, with few exceptions, were manned by the same social group. Another example is Hajji Muhammad Husayan Khan, Grand Vizier from 1819 until 1823. He was a merchant by trade and came from a *kadkhuda* family in Isfahan, where he himself became *kalantar*. He won distinction by improving the *bazar* and building *karavanserais* and for his "sagacity and ingenuity in the handling of affairs and in bargaining with the landowners and his capacity to derive advantage from everything," and the Qajars therefore appointed him governor of Isfahan and afterwards gave him posts in the central administration. His son Abdullah Khan

Aminu'd-Davleh, succeeded him as governor of Isfahan and as
Grand Vizier for two periods (1823-25, 1828-34) (Fasa'i 1972,
p. 167; Malcolm 1828 II, p. 183; Ouseley 1819 III, p. 22;
on the *kalantars* of Kirman see Busse 1972, p. 291).

Both the Qajar state and the patrician families derived
advantages from this cooperation. The families entered the
imperial administration because office meant wealth, influence and the opportunity to protect and perhaps extend their
local power base. The state for its part made use of the
administrative experience of the families and their local
influence to control the towns and solve the innumerable
disputes in the provinces.

The influence of the patrician families was not due to
their wealth alone, but also to their ability to protect the
home town form the imperial tax-collectors and governors
and from the tribes. They were also expected to bring the
town material advantages and to provide local disputes with
reasonable solutions. As long as they lived up to these ex-
pectations, their local positions were seldom affected
crucially by the fate of individual family members at court.
Hajji Ibrahim's family may serve again as an illustration.
For it succeeded, despite the fall of the head of the family,
in keeping its position in Shiraz. One of the Hajji's sons,
Mirza Ali Akbar - later known by his honorary title,
Qavamu'l-Mulk - was appointed *kalantar* in 1812 (Fasa'i 1972,
p. 142), and he consolidated his position over the following years by, among other things, marrying into the family
which commanded the town's garrison of *mazandarani* troops.[18]
A common enmity towards Mushiru'l-Mulk,[19] who held the office of *vazir* for the governors of Fars for many years,
linked him with the Qashqa'i *ilkhan*, and to strengthen this
overlap of interests he had some of his children marry into
the family of the *ilkhan*. This type of alliance between a
khan and a patrician family was of course unacceptable from
the point of view of the state, and the governor of Fars,
Husayn Ali Farman-Farma (a son of Fath Ali Shah), ordered
an immediate divorce (Fasa'i 1972, pp. 193, 206 f).

Qavam was involved in numerous disputes with the governors and their *vazirs*, because of tax demands, among other things. In 1843 he led a deputation of local patricians to Tehran in order to have an unpopular governor dismissed, and on several occasions he mobilized his clients and allies among the tribal *khans* to back up his demands with force (Fasa'i 1972, pp. 219, 274). When Husayn Khan Nizamu'd-Davleh, governor from 1844 until 1848, tried to break his power by divesting him of the office of *kalantar*, this was the cue for a full-scale armed uprising which led to the dismissal of the governor (Fasa'i 1972, p. 283).

The governors were in fact in a situation where, in order to be able to govern at all, they had to choose between the support of Qavam or that of his rivals among the local patricians. This did not mean that Qavam only acted to defend local interests against the state. For example, he refused to support Farman-Farma when the latter attempted, on the death of Fath Ali Shah, to seize the throne from the heir designate, and thus contributed to the stabilization of the Qajar state (Fasa'i 1972, p. 233). During the 1856 war with Great Britain he again demonstrated his loyalty by undertaking - along with other potentates in Fars - to pay for and organize supplies to the Iranian troops in the Gulf region (Fasa'i 1972, p. 327).

Qavam's career came to an end when he was appointed vice-administrator of the *auqaf* of the Imam Riza shrine in 1865, which meant in effect that he was sent into honourable exile in Mashhad. However, both the office of *kalantar* and the honorary title passed to his son Ali Muhammad (Fasa'i 1972, pp. 343, 348 ff). The British doctor C. J. Wills, who was attached to the British telegraph service in Iran for several years, and who did service in Shiraz among other places, described him as "the only local man of real power in the province of Fars" (Wills 1891, p. 272), and emphasized his great popularity, which was due not least to the fact that Qavam II and his family, in accordance with tradition, used their offices to defend local merchant and

landowner interests and to encourage public-service initia-
tives (for example, the *kadkhudas* of Shiraz had their economic subsidies increased, road surfaces were improved and
the roof of the *bazar* was repaired, and Qavam paid out of
his own pocket for repairs and extensions to the city water
supply) (Fasa'i 1972, pp. 398, 419). Apart from his position as *kalantar* Qavam also held the office of sub-governor
of Darab and Laristan, and shortly before his death in 1882
he became vice-governor of all Fars (Fasai 1972, pp. 357,
382). At the same time his brother Fath Ali Khan, who had
done service in the central administration and had held the
post of Grand Vizier, was appointed *vazir* of Fars. The
state made further use of Qavam's influence as a counter-
weight to the Qashqa'i tribe and appointed him *khan* of a
newly-established confederation, the Khamseh, which com-
prised among others the Inanlu, Baharlu and Baseri tribes
(Fasa'i 1972, p. 387). The control of the warriors of
these tribes helped the family to defend its local position
during the uneasy years of the Constitutional Revolution and
the First World War.

As we have seen, the Qajars succeeded in eliminating
rival leaders, breaking the power of the *khans* and rendering
the state independent of the nomad military potential. They
reconquered part of the lost Iranian territories, avoided
exhausting wars of succession and built up an administration which was as efficient as Iranian conditions permitted.
Where the 18th-century wars fought for imperial power had
wrought great destruction in Iran, the Qajars established a
state of peace and order which contributed to demographic
and - at least in the first half of the 19th century - economic growth (this cannot be quantified, but on the basis of
the available source material there can be no doubt about
the general tendency of developments) (cf. statements by
Malcolm 1828 I, p. 97; Malcolm 1829 II, p. 518 f; Ouseley
1819 III, p. 22.

The Qajar state can thus arguably be said to have lived
up to the hopes which Hajji Ibrahim, on behalf of the patrician group, had placed in it. Nevertheless it is possible
to trace the beginnings of a conflict of interests between
this group and the state from the reign of Muhammad Shah onwards, - a conflict whose roots lay in the consolidation of
state power itself. For the Qajar efforts towards centralization did not stop with the elimination of warlords and the
subjugation of the *khans*. Throughout the whole of the 19th
century a gradual increase in the functions of the state
took place at the expense of those groups who had formerly
fulfilled these functions and thereby gained income and
social status (Algar 1969, p. 170). It affected the patrician group that the secular courts, which dispensed customary law (*urf*), increased their scope at the expense of the
religious courts, which were administrated by the *ulama* ,
and that the governors - not always successfully, however -
attempted to limit the power of the great families in their
home bases (at the same time the state was able, not least
because of the improvements in communications afforded by
the telegraph, to prevent the governors from developing
into semi-autonomous local rulers) (on the telegraph see
Litten 1920, pp. 3 ff, 287 f; Curzon 1892 II, pp. 607-16).

The constant lack of funds of the Qajars also gave rise
to increasing conflict. Under Aqa Muhammad and Fath Ali
Shah, both of whom were notorious for their miserliness and
greed (Malcolm 1829 II, pp. 308, 480 ff), the incomes of
the state exceeded its expenses, but under Muhammad Shah
the situation was reversed. The policy of centralization,
the many campaigns and the maintenance of the *nizam-e jadid*
stretched the modest economic resources of the Qajar state
to the breaking point - and finally beyond it.

The few figures which are available indicate that the
military swallowed a very great proportion of the money
without the Qajars succeeding at any point in creating an
efficient pay system.[20] Mutiny and refusal of duty were a
recurrent problem. In 1847 the troops who were scheduled

to go off to quell an uprising in Khurasan refused to march
before they had been paid at least part of the pay that was
due to them (the money was procured through loans from some
merchants) (Lambton 1971, p. 333). In order to make a living
at all most soldiers had to work on the side as craftsmen,
porters, etc. In the field they lived off the land, in accordance with tradition, and they did so with great thorough-
ness to compensate for the lack of pay (e.g. Sheil 1856, p.
392; Fraser 1840 I, pp. 131, 146, 159, II, pp. 236, 287, 296,
301; Greaves 1965 (I), p. 44). Campaigns against rebellious
local rulers often assumed the aspect of sheer plundering
raids (e.g. Layard 1846, p. 31 ff), and when the army moved
from Azarbayjan to Tehran in 1834 to install Muhammad Shah
on the throne, it left the country between Qazvin and Tehran,
according to Fraser, like "a desert" (Fraser 1840 II, p. 296).
The inhabitants of one of the villages affected told him:

> "First came Imaum Verdee Meerza (the rebellious
> general) and his army, and he took what he lik-
> ed; then came Mahomed Shah's troops and licked
> up his leavings; so we all took to the hills,
> and you will not find another village with peo-
> ple in it up to the gates of Casveen."

(Fraser 1840 II, p. 301)

Another Englishman who came to Hamadan in 1840 in the wake
of the army described how the city "looked as if it had been
taken and sacked in war" (quoted in Curzon 1892 I, p.
608). Theoretically, the areas which had suffered in this
way had the right to compensation in the form of tax relief,
but the economically pressed Qajars often ignored this tradition (Fraser 1840 II, pp. 237, 287).

The Qajar state constantly attempted to increase taxes
and find new sources of income. The tax system which they
had inherited from their predecessors was complex and characterized by arbitrariness (on taxation practices in general see Lambton 1953). Special rules varied from region to
region and for different crops, property relations and irrigation methods; but on the whole the situation was as follows. State income came partly from *maliyat*, i.e. the

regular, specified taxes on agriculture, trade and the
profits made by craftsmen, and partly from a large number
of extraordinary taxes, duties and requisitions which were
levied for specific purposes (e.g. to cover expenses for
the Shah's coronation, wars etc.). These extra taxes
amounted at the beginning of the 19th century to about the
same as *maliyat* (Malcolm 1829, p. 479 f). Tax-gathering
was farmed out locally to a great extent, and the local
concessionaires had a traditional claim to a certain a-
mount of "surplus" (*madakhil*) which was to be used to give
"gifts" to influential officials. This surplus was made up
by the levying of special duties for the defrayment of administrative expenses and the like (Lambton 1953, p. 144).
A large proportion of the tax gathered never reached Tehran, but was used locally to pay garrisoned troops, to
finance various public facilities etc. The tax burden
weighed heaviest on the peasants. According to Kinneir
they paid 2/3 of the *maliyat* (Kinneir 1813, p. 47), and
their share of the extraordinary taxes was hardly less.

During the time of Fath Ali Shah there was a general
doubling of *maliyat* from 10 to 20% of the harvest yield,[21]
and throughout the whole century the extraordinary taxes
also rose sharply. Not surprisingly, tax-gathering met
with opposition and obstruction at all levels and therefore often had to be carried out with armed support (Fraser
1825, p. 211 f; Malcolm 1829 II, p. 474; Lambton 1967, p.
57; Lambton 1953, p. 145).

The Qajars also extorted large amounts from their
governors and officials in the form of "gifts"[22] or
fines.[23] In return the governors squeezed more money out
of the local tax concessionaires and the wealthy, who subsequently increased their demands on their subordinates.
In the last analysis it was the peasants who had to pay
for the Qajar efforts to squeeze money out of the upper
classes. It cannot be specified in more detail how much
extra the primary taxpayers actually had to pay in the form
of administrative expenses, arbitrarily established "gifts"

and sheer extortion, but in general the situation must have
been one of severe economic strain. Percy Sykes estimated
that at the turn of the century 450,000 *tumans* were levied
in Kirman, although the province was formally assessed at
only 315,000 (Sykes 1902, p. 47).

The Qajars had to concede local and temporary tax relief in cases of drought, locust swarms and other catastro-
phes (e.g. Fasa'i 1972, pp. 135, 201; Goldsmid 1876, p.
369), and although it was rarely noticed by contemporary
European observers, they also made investments to promote
production, first and foremost in irrigation schemes, and
they tried to coax or force local landowners to do the
same (e.g. Fasa'i 1972, p. 278 f; Sykes 1902, p. 69 f;
Goldsmid 1876, pp. 86, 90, 99 f, 151 f, 177, 181, 204).
But in general Iranian agriculture, for both social and
ecological reasons, was unable to increase production to
keep up with the tax burden (c.f. Christensen 1982, pp.
607-625). The peasants reacted to the increasing tax
squeeze with passive resistance. They could, for example,
conceal part of the harvest yield, flee from the tax-collectors or emigrate abroad - which of course increased
the tax burden on those who stayed behind (e.g. Fasa'i
1972, p. 389; Ouseley 1819 II, p. 424; Wills 1891, p. 131;
Lambton 1953, p. 171). By the end of the 19th century
emigration from Azarbayjan and Khurasan in particular had
reached considerable proportions, as the poverty-stricken
peasants and craftsmen could quite easily find work in
industry in Russian Transcaucasia and on the great rail-
way schemes in Transcaspia. This emigration was not permanent, and most of them returned home when they had earn-
ed a certain amount of money. According to the official
statistics (which do not include the extensive illegal
emigrations) 100,000 Iranians left for Russia in 1908;
at the same time 87,000 returned, bringing with them not
only about 6 million roubles, but also new practical skills
and political experience (Entner 1965, p. 59 ff).

A gloomier aspect of the Qajar economic policy was
that it exacerbated situations of food scarcity. With a
negligible surplus it was difficult for agriculture to mi-
tigate the effects of drought and crop failure. In the e-
vent of a short-term, local drought the peasants could usually pull through by living on fruit, while on the other
hand the poor in the cities were struck a severe blow at
once when there was a corn scarcity, not least because the
governors and their officials often kept the public corn
stores closed so they could capitalize on the rising prices
(c.f. the description of the famine in Shiraz, Wills 1891,
p. 251 ff). Longer periods of drought, however, had incal-
culable consequences. For the two years between 1869 and
1871 winter rain failed to fall over most of the country,
qanats and rivers dried up, the crop failed and cattle
died. The subsequent famine, which was accompanied by e-
pidemics of typhus, dysentery and cholera, cost hundreds of
thousands of human lives. There are no hard statistics on
the catastrophe, but all accounts from the 1870's speak of
wholly or partly depopulated towns and deserted villages,
whose streets were "literally strewn with dead men's bones"
(Goldsmid 1876, pp. 95 f, 341 f, 369). The effects were
worst in the eastern provinces.[24]

In short, Iranian agriculture could not in the long
run support the expenses connected with attempts at reconquest and centralization, and the Qajar state therefore had
to keep looking for supplementary sources of income. In
the second half of the 19th century the state sold large
portions of the crown land, *khaliseh*, which the first
Qajars had amassed either by purchase or confiscation from
rebels and tax debtors (Lambton 1953, pp. 147, 152 f;
also Lambton, "Khalisa" in EI/2). But first and foremost
the efforts of the Qajar state were directed against the
merchants. It had always been state practice to cover
urgent expenses by borrowing money from the great, wealthy
merchants, but gradually, as the state in the time of
Muhammad Shah began to prove unwilling to pay these loans

back, it became more difficult for it to find lenders.
Muhammad Shah then tried to establish a form of credit
system, where he allowed soldiers, civil servants, etc.
to be paid with *barats*, i.e. debit notes which in theory
were to be honoured by the treasuries of the individual
provinces. As he had soon issued more *barats* than there
was backing for, the result was that only influential people could have any hope of having the notes honoured. They
therefore became objects of speculation: rich merchants
and leading officials bought them up for a pittance, as
they calculated that they themselves would be able to have
them wholly or partly honoured and thus make a large profit
(Sheil 1856, p. 386; Lambton 1971, p. 332 f). On the death
of Muhammad Shah all outstanding *barats* were declared inva-
lid - to the great relief of the Treasury, but at the expense of many buyers, who lost considerable sums.[25]

Another source of bitterness among both great and
small merchants was the Qajar taxation of trade (Issawi
1971, pp. 76, 80; also art. "Kharadj" in EI/2). At the
beginning of the 19th century Iran was still "a country
which has very little inland trade" (Waring 1807, p. 76),
as the individual regions were on the whole self-sufficient
as regards basic goods. Lightweight and costly luxury
goods were transported via a network of caravan routes con-
necting Iran on one side with the Central Asiatic *khan*ates,
Herat and Qandahar (and through these with India), and on
the other the Ottoman state. On Qajar territory the desert town of Yazd was the nodal point for long-distance
trade, where a large proportion of the goods which com-
prised the contribution of the Iranian towns to trade were
gathered together (Waring 1807, p. 76). These were above
all various textiles, the production of which kept a large
number of craftsmen employed in, among other places, Isfahan, Kashan, Yazd, Kirman and Rasht. Both the everyday
local trade and the caravans paid a duty at all the larger towns. At Shiraz it amounted, formally at least, to
2.5% of the value. Thus before a caravan reached its

destination the total duty could run to 30% more of the
value of the goods (Waring 1807, p. 80; Issawi 1971, p.
365). The modest proportions of trade, along with the
fact that the collection of duties was farmed out, had the
effect, according to Waring, that "the trade of Persia is
comparatively of very little advantage to the state; it
adds but little to the revenue" (Waring 1807, p. 77).

But this changed as the Qajar state was drawn into the
European international market and the strategic conflict
between Russia and Great Britain. Both great powers sought
to promote their own trade and investments in the hope of
gaining political influence. In the first half of the
19th century it was especially the British-dominated trade
in the Gulf and Southern Iran which grew (Issawi 1971, p.
83 f), while in the second half of the century Russia's
trade with the northern provinces saw faster growth, a-
mong other reasons because the construction of the Transcaucasian and Transcaspian railways gave easier access to
the Iranian market, and because the Russian state granted
solid state subsidies to a number of commodities (e.g.
sugar) to make them more competitive on the market (Entner
1965, pp. 24, 70). It has been estimated that in the period from 1800 until 1914 there was an overall twelvefold
increase in the value of the Qajar state's foreign trade
(Issawi 1971, p. 130 ff).

In order to favour her own trade and protect it against
arbitrary taxation Russia had, at the peace settlement of
Turkmanchay (1828), stipulated that a once-for-all duty of
5% of the value should be paid on all goods which crossed
the Russo-Iranian border (Hurewitz 1965). Great Britain
and a number of other European nations eventually achieved
similar terms. This meant that while European merchants
got off with a once-for-all duty and could then trade free-
ly anywhere in Iran, the Iranian merchants still had to
pay duties in all the larger towns and had to resign themselves to arbitrary increases. European interprises could
therefore gradually take over an ever-increasing portion of

the trade in Iran. In several sectors the home merchants
managed to keep up their positions in full, but more and
more were forced to seek foreign protection or citizen-
ship to remain competitive. Others were reduced to the
status of agents for European concerns (Issawi 1971, pp.
80 f, 103 f).

As trade grew the interest of the Qajar state in tax-
gathering grew too. In the course of the 1870's and 1880's
it was brought under centralized control - i.e. concessions
were granted by officials of the central administration instead of local potentates and governors; and in 1898 Nasiru'd-Din Shah went a stage further by completely abolishing
the concessions system and letting the state take care of
direct administration. This was accomplished with the help
of a group of Belgian advisers. The result was a marked
rise in state income - and a more strained relationship
with the merchants. In their opinion the Belgians favoured foreign and non-Muslim merchants, and the administration
of the tariffs became a symbol of the growing foreign influence which was threatening the very existence of the
Iranian merchants (Algar 1969, p. 226 f; Litten 1920, p.
240 ff; Sheikholeslami 1978, p. 233 f).

The subsistence of Iranian craftsmen was also threatened by trade developments. Cheap British and Russian cotton
was flooding Iran to the detriment of the weavers and other
craftsmen who had been employed in traditional textile production. According to a report on Isfahan from the close
of the 1870's the number of weavers in the city had fallen
by no less than 80%, and the author added: "About one-
twentieth of the needy widows of Isfahan raised their children by spinning thread for the weavers; they have all
perished" (Quoted in Issawi 1971, p. 281). The report
mentions that there had been 1250 workshops in Fath Ali
Shah's time producing silk; of these there were 12 left
(Issawi 1971, p. 281). This was an extreme case. But even
if the recession in general was not quite so catastrophic,
craftsmanship was hard pressed by competition from the im-

ported industrial goods, not only on the Iranian market,
but also on the traditional export markets in Central Asia.
a few crafts experienced vigorous growth precisely because
their products could be sold internationally. This was
above all true of hand-knotted carpets, but it was indicative of developments that even here European concerns increasingly took over the financing of production and distribution (Goldsmid 1876, pp. 187, 190, 199 f; Litten 1920,
pp. 92 ff, 218 ff; Issawi 1971, p. 301 ff).

European concerns also began to buy up - and invest in
the production of - Iranian raw materials like cotton, silk,
opium, dried fruit etc. (Litten 1920, pp. 93, 186 f; Issawi
1971, p. 226 f; Entner 1965, pp. 62 f, 73 f). Yet it would
be far from true to say that Iranian agriculture was all at
once realigned towards production for the world market.
Innovations were concentrated in Northern Iran, where expansion of the cultivated area and a transformation from
self-sufficiency to market-orientated production took place
in certain regions which, thanks to the Transcaucasian and
Transcaspian railways and the steamship connections across
the Caspian Sea, had easy access to the Russian market. In
the great majority of places agriculture was affected to a
very small extent, i.e. the effect of the transformation
was in the first instance to accentuate the differences
between the relatively privileged northern provinces and
the rest of the country.[26]

Besides the income from customs duties, the international market - stimulated by the special status of Iran in
the Russo-British struggle for influence - could offer new
sources of income in the form of loans and the sale of concessions.

In Europe imaginative and ill-founded ideas about the
natural wealth of Iran and the Iranian market were rife,
and in the beginning British capital in particular was in-
terrested in making investments (Brockway 1941). But after
most of the major private concessions - first and foremost
the Reuter concession (1872) and the Tobacco Regie (1890) -

had failed following Iranian opposition, the desire to invest became more subdued. True, a number of less ambitious
concessions were established, but this was because they were
supported by the British and Russian states, which considered them politically important. Examples of this were the
founding of the British Imperial Bank and the Russian Banque
d'Escompte, both of which functioned as instruments of great-
power policies, and the strategically and commercially important road projects in Northern and Southern Iran (i.e.
the Russian Anzali-Tehran, Qazvin-Hamadan and Julfa-Tabriz
roads and the British Arabistan and Bakhtiyari roads) (for
a summary of concessions see Litten 1920).

Regarded as sources of income the concessions were on
the whole a disappointment to the Qajar state. The two foreign banks were, however, willing to grant certain loans and
increasingly took over the traditional role of the merchants
as lenders to the state in acute situations (the Russian
bank was similarly willing to lend money to the Qajar princes and other economically distressed but influential private individuals).[27]

Compared with Egypt and the Ottoman state, for example,
the Qajar state on the whole received modest amounts of foreign capital - during the period up to 1914 hardly more than
£26,000,000, out of which a little over £7,500,000 consisted
of various short and long term loans (Christensen 1975, p.
82 f) - yet the concessions and loans must not only be evaluated on the strength of the amounts involved, but also on
the basis of their political consequences. For example, the
large Russian loans of 1900 and 1902 were granted on terms
which severely limited, at least formally, the political
freedom of action of the Qajar state (Entner 1965, p. 48 f;
Kazemzadeh 1968, pp. 324 ff, 362 ff). The economic infil-
tration of Iran by Russia was characterized on the whole
by a state-directed aggressiveness and determination which
convinced the British that the central power in Iran was
falling completely under Russian domination (Greaves 1965).
To protect their position in Southern Iran they therefore

began increasingly to expand their contacts with local
rulers there, among others with Zill us-Sultan (the son of
Nasir ud-Din Shah, governor of Isfahan and until 1887 over-
lord of large areas in Southern Iran), with the Bakhtiyari
khans and the *Shaykh* of Muhammareh (Garthwaite 1972;
Greaves 1959, p. 150 f; further details on the relations
with the *Shaykh* of Muhammareh can be found in Busch 1967).
In this way they contributed to a weakening of the control
of the sourthern provinces which the Qajars had struggled
laboriously for throughout the course of the century.

The political significance of the concessions lay in
the fact that they, like the Belgian customs administration,
appeared as symbols of the European penetration which was
threatening to annihilate the traditional way of life in
the cities, and thus fuelled the opposition to the Qajars.

Considered from a narrowly economic point of view, the
most tangible effect of the international market on Iran
was to create inflation. The Iranian monetary system, based
exclusively on silver, deteriorated sharply in the second
half of the 19th century, and particularly in the 1890's,
because of the international drop in the price of silver
(Avery & Simmons 1980). The consequences of this inflation
are difficult to assess, because large sectors of the economy still only had a limited interface with the market;
but it is clear at least that there was an attrition of
state income[28] and merchant capital and a rise in food
prices which hit the town-dwellers hard and occasioned an
increasing number of hunger revolts (Issawi 1971, p. 348).

Unlike the peasants, who, as mentioned above, reacted
only with passive resistance to punitive taxes and other
forms of repression,[29] the town-dwellers in Iran had a
tradition of organized, violent - if as a rule bloodless -
revolts. In a few cases the patrician group stood behind
the risings and exploited their prestige to mobilize the
population's resistance to governors, *vazirs*, tax-gatherers
and other unpopular representatives of the state (e.g.

Fasa'i 1972, pp. 250, 283; McNeill 1910, p. 146, f; Abbot
1857, p. 184). In other cases (and this was true of more
than the recurring hunger revolts alone) the initiative
came from the "menu peuple" of the *bazar*, and in such cases
the patricians were often obliged to fall into line if they
wanted to retain their esteem and influence. In 1839 the
bazar craftsmen in Shiraz started an uprising against the
city's hated garrison of *Azarbayjani* troops, and the patricians, including the *ulama*, came out on the side of the
rebels and moreover undertook the formal leadership of, and
thus responsibility for, the revolt (Qavam ul-Mulk, the
most influential citizen in Shiraz, had gone on a pilgrimage in order not to have to defend the representatives of
the governor of Fars, Faridun Mirza, a brother of Muhammad
Shah (Fasai 1972, p. 263 ff).

Apart from the *Babi* revolt (1848-51)[30] these city
revolts were aimed at tyrannical and unpopular individuals
(the hunger revolts were similarly aimed at persons who,
rightly or wrongly, were suspected of hoarding corn to
speculate in prices) and not against the state as such.
In other words, it was not the authority of the Shah but
the honesty of his officials which was being questioned,
so as a rule the Shah could pour oil on troubled waters
without extensive use of military power by sacrificing the
individuals in question. When a hunger revolt broke out
in Tehran in the spring of 1861, Nasir ud-Din Shah had the
city's *kalantar* executed and the *kadkhudas* bastinadoed
(Eastwick 1864 I, p. 287 ff), which did not solve the
problem of supplies, but demonstrated the Shah's willingness to see justice done to the full without regard to
rank or eminence. In 1878 the powerful governor of Kirman
similarly fell from office as a consequence of a hunger revolt (Busse 1872, p. 293).

In pursuance of the discussion which was touched upon
in the introduction, the role of the *ulama* in this context
requires a comment. There are innumerable examples of the
direct or indirect involvement of the *ulama* in uprisings

(e.g. in 1877 the *ulama* of Qum led a rising in protest a-
gainst raising of taxes, Bassett 1887, p. 284), and it was
normal practice that the insurrectionists gathered in *ulama*
homes or in mosques to plan the uprising.[31] But there are
also numerous examples of the *ulama* providing support to
the state and its local representatives in quelling uprisings (it must in this context be remembered that the
ulama - for example by handing over Mashhad to Fath Ali
Shah - had also actively supported the Qajar state in its
founding phase) (Watson 1866, pp. 358 ff, 377; Fasa'i 1972,
p. 103 f). The *ulama* enjoyed a geniune autonomy in relations
with the state, by virtue of, among other things, the independent income they had from *auqaf* and *khums*, so that they
could occasionally take the liberty of criticizing the state.
But for those who would assert that there existed a constant
tension between the *ulama* - the guardians of the law and
morality and the defenders of the underdogs - and the tyrannical state, it is a source of embarrassment that many *ulama*
who, like Aqa Najafi in Isfahan, often attacked the state
in no uncertain terms, at the same time had no qualms about
using their wealth and position in the speculative buying-
up of corn or otherwise enriching themselves at the expense
of the underprivileged in society (e.g. Algar 1969, p. 14 f).
A British diplomat[32] at the turn of the century called the
ulama

> "the worst robbers in the state. Being admini-
> strators of the law, they are gradually acquiring
> vast landed property, swamping village after vil-
> lage. Money will buy them all (....)"
>
> (Gwynn 1929 I, p. 296 f).

This cannot be explained away by the statement that "on occasion venality overcame religion (Algar 1969, p. 16). The
ulama in question at any rate saw nothing morally reprehens-
ible in their activities. The key to understanding the attitudes and activities of the *ulama* in the 19th century must
in my opinion be sought in their close ties, through wealth,
status and family bonds, with the patrician group (This
point is also made by Floor 1980, p. 74 f). They shared

the norms of this group and its views on the state and society, and their economic transactions and eternal power
struggles were typically patrician activities. The pro-
tracted conflict between Sayyid Muhammad Baqir Shafti, the
de facto ruler of Isfahan in the first half of the 19th
century, and the successive governors of the city, sprang
rather from Shafti's position as a patrician than from a
legally or doctrinally determined opposition to the state.
As a respected member of the ulama Shafti of course enjoyed special authority, but his power in the city also depended on wealth and the control of a local militia of
lutis. For this reason too Manuchihr Khan was in the end
able to loosen his stranglehold on the city by secular means
(Shafti's son and successor, Aqa Najafi remained, however,
one of the most powerful men in Isfahan) (Algar 1969, pp.
59 f, 108 ff. Also p. 57 f).

The ulama, like the other patricians, often had grounds
for dissatisfaction with the Qajar state on concrete issues,
but their practice shows that they fundamentally accepted
not only the existence of the state but also its authority.
The enemies of the ulama in the 19th century were not the
Qajars, but the Sufis and the Babis (Malcolm 1829 II, p.
414 ff).

Local insurrections, hunger revolts and the like had
no great need of ideological legitimation. If the pater-
nalistic state failed in its duties to its subjects, disturbances and protests were time-honoured means of di-
recting the attention of the Shah to the abuses. Special
sanction from the ulama was rarely necessary.[33)]

It was otherwise with the protest movement which began
with the Tobacco Protest of 1891-92 and culminated in the
Constitutional Revolution of 1905-06. As this movement
gradually developed into a deliberate attempt to curtail
the power of the Qajar state and establish a new political
system, its need for ideological legitimation grew. Since
the movement was composed of heterogeneous elements, it

took its ideological legitimation from various sources. The
existing literature on the subject often stresses the small
groups of European-inspired reformers and revolutionaries,
but their significance has, as far as I can see, been over-
rated. The great majority of participants in the protest
movement acted on the basis of a world picture defined in
religious terms and appealed to the authority which indis-
putably stood above the Shah, namely Islam. It was of
course the most important duty of the *ulama* to decide what
was in accordance with the principles of Islam. The *ulama*
in opposition argued that the Shah, by practising tyranny
and giving concessions and other privileges to the Europeans, had betrayed Muslim society and broken the Sacred Law,
and that it was therefore the duty of the faithful to reject his authority.

The immediate cause of the protest was the granting
of a monopoly on the buying, distribution and export of
Iranian-produced tobacco to a British concern by Nasir
ud-Din Shah during his European tour in 1889. Unlike previous concessions (such as the building of the telegraph
system) this monopoly quite obviously threatened the existence of many Iranian merchants and retailers. The
protest followed the traditional pattern, which has been
described briefly above. The merchants affected attempted
to have the concession revoked by writing petitions, and
when this did not help they mobilized the townspeople in
Shiraz, Tehran, Tabriz, Isfahan and Mashhad in massive de-
monstrations, closed the *bazars* etc., with the support of
the *ulama* in 1891.[34] In Isfahan they organized a total
boycott on tobacco, and the boycott was spread country-
wide by a *fatva* issued (or at least endorsed) by the most
eminent *mujtahid* of the time, Hasan Shirazi, who was stay-
ing at Samarra, far beyond the reach of the Shah; thus
the whole economic base for the monopoly was jeopardized.

The Qajar state, which was under British pressure to
keep the concession in force, at first tried to muffle the
protests by arresting leading agitators and having soldiers

disperse the demonstration processions. But the Tobacco
Revolt was nation-wide, unlike previous risings - because
the abuse, i.e. the monopoly, was nation-wide - and the
Qajar state did not possess an apparatus of repression
which was capable of restraining the population of all the
major cities. Moreover, the loyalty of the army was crumb-
ling. Large numbers of soldiers were, as mentioned before,
partly employed in civilian trades and therefore had emoti-
onal ties with the *bazar*, quite apart from the fact that
they shared the world picture of the rebels. In many cases
they refused to open fire on the demonstrators. Faced with
the threat of a full-scale armed uprising in Azarbayjan the
Shah, after various forms of delaying tactics, in the end
had to face defeat and annul the concession (for details
see Lambton 1965 and Keddie 1966 (a)).

The uprising had been staved off, but the authority of
the state had suffered a serious blow. Nasir ud-Din Shah
had invested prestige and soldiery and had still suffered
a conspicuous defeat at the hands of the opposition. It
was significant of the situation as a whole that he was
assassinated in 1896 by a ruined *bazari*.[35]

Those *ulama* who had come forward as leaders of the
protest - among others Hasan Ashtiyani (Tehran), Aqa Najafi
(Isfahan) and Aqa Javad (Tabriz) - can in no way be described as liberal or pro-reform in the European sense.
They were respected and influential members of the locally
entrenched power elite, and the fact that they attacked
the Qajars for tyranny and the betrayal of Islam marked a
rupture between the Qajars and those groups which had contributed to putting them in power.

The annulment of the concession did nothing to relieve
the tensions which had caused the rupture and despite the
attempts of the Qajars to play off rival *ulama* against one
another the opposition continued in the following years to
agitate against the Belgian customs administration (whose
unpopularity was the cause of extensive disturbances in

Tabriz in 1903), the Russian loans in 1900 and 1902 and the
introduction of new customs tariffs in 1903. This agitation
was no longer directed against individual abuses, but was
critical of the Qajar state in general and began to demand
an institutionalized limitation of the power of the Shah.
At the end of 1905 the *sadr-e azam* Ayn ud-Davleh, who belonged to the Qajar family, began a series of harassments
and abuses of the merchants and *ulama* in the hope of
frightening the agitators. But victory of the Tobacco Revolt had given the opposition confidence in its own powers,
and it responded to Ayn ud-Davleh's repression with a number of increasingly wide-ranging protest activities in
Tehran, Tabriz, Shiraz, Isfahan and Rasht (for example the
closing of *bazars* and large scale *basts* in the gardens of
the British legation). In Tehran, where the main confron-
tation took place, the opposition was led by two *ulama*,
Muhammad Tabataba'i and Abdullah Bihbihani, with the full
support of the influential *ulama* in the *atabat* (the Shi'i
holy cities in Iraq).

The Qajar state attempted to silence the protests by
force of arms, but as had been the case in 1891 this only
led to an intensification of the disturbances and a more
vehement tone in the agitation (for example the Qajars were
now directly compared with the Ummayyads, the murderers of
the martyr Husayn, figures who occupied a position of special loathing in the Shi'i world picture). The political
claims, too, were formulated more clearly in the course of
the conflict, and came to include the demand for the introduction of a constitution and the establishment of a
national assembly, the *majlis*. When the army proved in-
capable of containing the flood of disturbances the Qajar
state once again had to face defeat. On the 5th of August
1906 Muzaffar ud-Din Shah accepted the demand for a constitution and a *majlis*. He died immediately after signing
a hastily prepared interim constitution (which primarily
contained stipulations on the limitation of the power of
the Shah), and his son and successor, Muhammad Ali Shah,

made a last attempt, with Russian support, to quash the
opposition by force and reestablish Qajar rule. But it
was precisely his obvious dependence on Russia which helped
to unite the opposition, and the protagonists of the *majlis*
were able to round up support from groups as varied as the
Caucasian guerrillas on the one hand and the anti-Qajar
Bakhtiyari *khans* on the other. Muhammad Ali Shah's defeat
in the civil war of 1908-9 and subsequent exile marked in
effect the collapse of the Qajar state, even though it per-
sisted purely formally until 1925 (this brief account of
the Constitutional Revolution is based on Christensen 1975).

Because of great-power intervention, world war and
splits between moderate and radical groups the opposition
to the Qajars which had united on the question of the
majlis was unable to establish control of the whole country. Instead the successor to the Qajar state became the
centralized military dicatorship of Riza Shah, which in the
initial phase enjoyed the support of some of the patrician
group.

The Qajars had quite consistently pursued two political
aims which they defined and legitimated on the basis of historical traditions: centralization within the state and reconquest outwardly. Inadequate economic resources and a
number of external conditions were the reason why these aims
could no be realized in full, but the Qajars to a much greater extent than their predecessors, achieved control of the
tribes and local rulers, and of tax-gathering etc. In these
areas they paved the way for the strongly centralized Pahlavi state which followed.

The patricians and the merchants who had supported the
struggle of the Qajar state against *khans* and warlords gradually came to see their wealth and position threatened by
centralization, the growing burden of tax and the European
penetration which the Qajars¹ could not prevent and which
they often, with their lack of funds, directly encouraged.
The *ulama* intervened in the Tobacco Revolt and the Consti-

tutional Revolution to protect the established social structure - which in their eyes represented the God-given order
of society - against the innovations and abuses of the
Qajars. They supported the demand for a constitution and
a *majlis* - originally formulated by European-inspired reformers - because they regarded these institutions as
practical means of restraining the power of the Shah, of
righting a number of wrongs and of bringing a larger section
of the life of society into conformity with the stipulations
of the *sharia*. What they did not wish to do was introduce
European laws and forms of government (and several influential *ulama* withdrew from the opposition ranks and began
to combat the *majlis* actively when they realized that a constitution on European lines was incompatible with the
sharia)[36], nor did they wish to abolish the monarchy and
take over the government themselves (cf. Hairi 1977, p. 83
ff, for a discussion of the position of Muhammad Tabataba'i;
also Lambton 1974). The oppositional activities of the
ulama around the turn of the century were in short an expression of the old Iranian society's resistance to change.

In many respects the revolution of 1978-79 exhibited
similarities with the Constitutional Revolution: this was
true, for example, of the close cooperation between dis-
sident *ulama* and the *bazar*; of the agitation against the
tyranny of the state, godlessness and foreign influence;
of the mobilization of the townspeople in massive and per-
sistent protest marches, etc. But in the course of the in-
tervening years far-reaching structural changes had taken
place, as the opposition at the turn of the century had
feared, in Iranian society. The land reforms had driven
hundreds of thousands of destitutes *(mustazafin)* into the
towns, and the efficient centralization of the Pahlavi state,
along with the oil revenues, had eliminated the old patrician group and instead created new power elites whose existence was closely tied to that of the state. During this process the *ulama* had been cut off from influencing political
power in society as much as before. The state deliberately

attempted to marginalize them and did not flinch from ex-
posing them to direct persecution.

When the radical *ulama* - above all Ayatullah Khumayni -
entered actively into politics in the course of the 1960's
and 70's and called for the abolition of the monarchy and
the introduction of an Islamic republic, the social precon-
ditions were very different from those which had motivated
the *ulama* around the turn of the century. One can of course
speak of a certain continuity in so far as the *ulama* who
combated the Pahlavi state made use of traditional Shii
thinking, but the formulation of the new radical political
goals brought with it a radical reinterpretation of central
concepts in this thinking (as for example with the concept
of *vilayat-e faqih*). Both as regards political aims and
ideological legitimation the struggle of the *ulama* in the
1960's and 70's indicated a rupture with the political
practice of former times.

Notes:

1) Poverty-stricken and otherwise marginalized nomads
whose prospects of continuing to lead the nomadic
life were threatened had a tendency to attack caravans and raid permanent settlements. But that is
no reason to see the relationship between nomads
and settled communities as a general, absolute mutual antagonism. The borderline between the two ways
of life was fluid, and in the Iranian context the
terms "nomad" and "peasant", it must be said, apply
to opposite poles of a continuum of ways of life.
It must also be added that even "pure" nomads were
economically an integral part of the surrounding
society. Nor was tribal organization peculiar to
the nomads. Most tribes included nomadic, semi-
nomadic and settled groups; among these, however,
the nomads had a special status by virtue of their
military power (cf. the discussion in Masson Smith
1978).

2) *Tuyul*, briefly, means the transfer of the right to
levy tax in a given area for a stated period.

3) cf. Anthony Jenkinson's description of Safavid rule
at the beginning of the 1560's: "This land of Persia
is (...) devided into many kingdomes and provinces
(...) Every province hath his severall King, or Sultan,
all in obedience to the great Sophie (i.e. the Shah)."
R. Hakluyt 1598-1600, III, p. 35.

4) At Bashkent and Chaldiran the Ottomans inflicted
crushing defeats on the Aq Qoyunlu and Safavid caval-
ries respectively. In both cases the superior discipline of the Ottomans (and the consequent tactical
advantages) and their use of musket-bearing infantry
(janissaries) and artillery were decisive. The success of the Safavids to hold Azerbayjan in the long
run was due to their avoidance of pitched battles after Chaldiran and their use instead of scorched-earth
tactics to exacerbate the logistical problems the
Ottomans faced in the trackless mountains between
the two empires.

5) Among these slaves was Allahvardi Khan, who had won
favour in the struggles against the Uzbegs in Khurasan
and then took charge of the building up of Abbas I's
new army. He was rewarded with the governorship of
Fars. His son Imam Quli Khan inherited the office
and position of power, until Safi I had him executed
(Malmcolm 1829 II, p. 529 f, 571 f).

6)   Aqa Muhammad made use of marriage alliances, among
      other things, to this end. He belonged himself to
      the Qoyunlu clan, but could not himself marry (he
      had been castrated by political opponents at an ear-
      ly age); instead he had his nephew, Fath Ali, marry
      a daughter of a leading Devehlu *khan*. Later, as Shah,
      Fath Ali continued with this policy, and, among other
      things, had his son and the heir to the throne, Abbas
      Mirza, marry into the Devehlu clan.

7)   The *kalantar* was the official who was responsible for
      the administration of a town;his duties included, a-
      mong others, the allocation and levying of taxes,
      settling disputes, etc. The office was almost always
      occupied by members of influential local families, who
      made use of it to further local interests with the
      state (cf. A.K.S. Lambton, "Kalantar" in EI/2; Floor
      1971).

8)   His predecessor, Mirza Muhammad, who had been appoint-
      ed in Karum Khan's time, had left the town and enter-
      ed Qajar service as early as 1785, on the death of
      Ali Murad Khan-e Zand (Fasa'i 1972, p. 20).

9)   In particular the people of poor mountain areas like
      Nur and Larijan (in Mazandaran), Damghan, Farahan
      (the area between Arak and Qum) and Laristan (also
      well-known for its production of weapons) seem to
      have specialized in this way of earning a living.
      The bakhtiyaris of Zagros also supplied *tufangchis*
      of acknowledged skill (Fasa'i 1972, pp. 12, 14, 27,
      92, 134; Lambton 1953, p. 138; Kinneir 1813, pp. 46,
      83).

10)   Nadir Shah's armies consisted mainly but not exclusi-
      vely of tribal cavalry, and his crushing defeats of
      the Ghilzay Afghans at Mehmandust and Zarghan were to
      a great extent due to artillery and *tufangchis*.

11)   Azarbayjan was dominated by great Turkish and Kurdish
      tribes such as the Shaqaqi, Javanshir (Qarabagh),
      Shahsavan (Ardabil) and Afshar (Urmiya); the Zagros
      region was divided among the tribes of the Qaraquzlu
      (Hamadan), Kalhur (Kirmanshah), Mamassani (Kazirun-
      Bihbihan), Qashqa'i and Bakhtiyari, whose territory
      also included Northern Khuzistan. Southern Khuzistan
      was dominated by the Arab Cha'b confederation under
      the shaykhs of Muhammareh. Khurasan was broadly di-
      vided between the *khan*ates of Quchan (the Zafaranlu
      tribe), Darreh Gaz (Chaperlu), Nishapur (Bayat), Tun-
      Tabas (Banu Shayban), Qayin, Turshiz (i.e. Kashmar),
      Turbat-e Haydari (Ishâq Khan), Sabzawar and Chaharan.
      Herat was ruled by a member of the Durrani family,
      Mashhad by descendants of Nadir Shah, while Marv -
      Iran's ancient bastion to the east - had fallen into
      Turcoman hands.

12) There is some obscurity about the circumstances behind the assassination. It is true that the sources
say that the culprits - some servants - acted on their
own initiative, but the events which took place in the
camp outside Shusha immediately after the murder, and
the uprisings which took place in the following months
in Azarbayjan indicate that the *khans* from the Kurdish Shaqaqi tribe were implicated (cf. Fasa'i 1972,
p. 74 and Malcolm 1829 II, p. 300).

13) Families from Farahan, one of the traditional *tufangchi*
areas, played a major role in the organization of the
new army (e.g. Mirza Abu'l-Qasim Farahani Qa'im Maqam).

14) Exhausting wars of succession had been a recurrent
problem for the earlier empires, but on this count
too the Qajar state, thanks to the army, achieved an
unheard-of stability, as it was no longer sufficient
for rivals to the heir designate to stir up dissatis-
fied tribal *khans*. As mentioned above, Fath Ali Shah
had subdued a couple of rivals; Muhammad Shah was
faced on his succession with only one rival, who was
quickly defeated; and Nasir ud-Din Shah not only mounted the throne without meeting opposition, but could
even allow himself to travel abroad several times.

15) The Herat incident is normally regarded as no more
than an appendix to the Russo-British struggle for
influence in Central Asia. The British in India were
at this juncture convinced that the Qajar state was
under strong Russian influence, and that the attack
on Herat was therefore part of the Russian "overall
plan" which would sooner or later culminate in an
assault on India (cf. Norris 1967, pp. 76 f, 118 f).
This assumption was uncritically taken over by later
historians, who also of course rely mostly on British
archive sources. It cannot be denied that the incident had international aspects and agents of the great
powers were active both in the Shah's camp and the
besieged city. But the real motive force behind the
Qajar attack was not in my opinion manipulation by
the great powers, but the historical tradition the
Qajar state was striving to live up to.

16) In a few cases the Qajars resorted to assassination
of particularly powerful and dangerous *khans*, e.g.
Murteza Quli Khan of the Qashqa'i in 1834 (Fasa'i
1972, pp. 223 ff) and the Bakhtiyari *ilkhan* Husayn
Quli Khan in 1882.

17) The term "patrician family", which I have borrowed
     from Bulliet, indicates "high social rank combined
     with local identification and loyalty". Without
     claiming that the social structure of Iran had re-
     mained completely unchanged since the Middle Ages,
     it seems to me that Bulliet's definition of the pa-
     trician group can also be used in speaking of the
     18th and 19th centuries: "a limited number of wealthy
     extended families whose dominance remained relatively
     stable over a period of many generations. The prestige
     and power of these families derived from one or more
     of three sources: landholding, trade, or religion."
     (R.W. Bulliet 1972, p. 20).

18) In order to keep the local rulers in check the Qajars
     would man the garrisons with troops from foreign pro-
     vinces, especially Azarbaydjan and Mazandaran (which
     provided the majority of the soldiers for the *nizam-e
     jadid*). This policy was extremely unpopular among
     the local townspeople and gave rise to numerous
     disturbances.

19) Mushiru'l-Mulk was himself an example of the continu-
     ity of the power of the great families. He occupied -
     apart from som interruptions - the position of *vazir*
     in Fars from 1829 until his death in 1847, when both
     the office and honorary title were taken over by his
     son, who held the office until 1876.

20) Of the total state income in 1850, which amounted to
     an estimated 3.2 million *tumans*, 1.2 million went to
     the army. In 1867-68 the corresponding figures were
     4.9 and 1.7 million respectively (Sheil 1856, pp.
     388 f; "Report on Persia 1867-68" quoted in Issawi
     1971, pp. 337, 364 f).

21) There were great local differences between the in-
     creases. In the Mahabad area (Kurdistan) tax rose
     from 1000 *tumans* in Aqa Muhammad's time to 25000
     tumans at the end of Fath Ali Shah's reign (Fraser
     1840 I, p. 112).

22) St. John estimated that the governor of Kirman in
     1870 was paying an annual tax of 200,000 *tumans* plus
     50,000 in gifts (Goldsmid 1876, p. 100).

23) Muhammad Nabi Khan, *vazir* to the governor of Fars
     from 1808 until 1810, was thus forced to pay 150,000
     tumans as a fine for negligence. A similar amount
     was extorted from a later *vazir*, Mushir ul-Mulk
     (Fasa'i 1972, pp. 132, 219 f).

24) The British mission sent to fix the boundaries in Sistan was informed that 24,000 had died in Mashhad after "every horse, mule, donkey, cat or rat in the town had been devoured". In Sabzawar there were said to be 10,000 survivors of a population of 30,000, while in Turbat-e Haydari there were 200 families left out of 1500 (Goldsmid 1876, pp. 353, 369, 373).

25) A.K.S. Lambton, for example, has studied a case where a merchant, by giving loans and buying up *barats* had collected a demand of about 200,000 *tumans* on the Fars administration. This money was never paid back, even though the British legation intervened on behalf of the merchant (Lambton 1971).

26) A contributory reason was the unwillingness of the peasants to reorganize production (export cultivation led, among other things, to rises in rents). Colonel Stewart noticed this when he came to the Turshiz area in Khurasan at the beginning of the 1880's, where opium poppies were cultivated: "When I told the people the price of opium in China had greatly fallen, they declared they were delighted, as they were forced by the owner of the village to grow opium, which pays him best, but the actual cultivator preferred to grow wheat". (Stewart 1911, p. 305).

27) The Banque d'Escompte, for example, granted loans to numerous landowners against security in the form of property. These properties thus came under the control of the Russian consuls, e.g. as regards taxation, i.e. the consuls undertook in effect to protect the landowners from state tax demands. The system was first adopted in the northern provinces, but it was later attempted to extend it to those areas in the south which, by the terms of the Russo-British Convention of 1907, belonged to Russia's "sphere of interest". Immediately before the First World War, the Banque d'Escompte thus took over the administration of Zill us-Sultan's properties in Isfahan (the latter had by this time given up his alliance with the British) the result of which was that about 150,000 peasants became partially exempted from Qajar control (this step was the occasion of an exacerbation of the already very tense Russo-British relationship in Iran). (Entner 1963, p. 15; Litten 1920, p. 118; IBZ V, no. 12).

28) There exists practically no reliable quantitative
material for the 19th century, and the following
figures are simply rough estimates: c. 1850 state
income amounted to about 3 million *tumans*, corre-
sponding to £1,600,000. At the end of the 1860's
the annual income had grown to 4,900,000 *tumans*
(£1,965,000). In 1888-89, i.e. just before the bot-
tom finally fell out of the silver market, the state
income of 5,500,000 *tumans* corresponded to only
(£1,600,000, and even though no figures are available for the 1890's the falling tendency (expressed
in pounds) must have been further intensified
(Sheil 1856, p. 388; Issawi 1971, p. 364; Curzon
1892 II, pp. 480 f).

29) Kazemi & Abrahamian 1978, applying Wolf's theory of
peasant revolt (cf. E.R. Wolf, *Peasant Wars of the
Twentieth Century*, New York 1973) seek an explanation
of the absence of major peasant risings in the fact
that among the Iranian peasant population there was
no "middle peasantry, that was able and willing to
challenge the power of the landlords". This explan-
tion is hardly adequate, but a more detailed discussion would fall outside the boundaries of the present
study.

30) On the basis of existing studies it is difficult to
relate the rise of the *Babi* movement to social developments in general. The fact that the movement's
prophet and founder, Sayyid Ali Muhammad, came from
a *Shirazi* merchant family, and that the movement primarily won support in the towns, has been interpreted
as a sign that the movement represented opposition to
the corrupt state and the reactionary *ulama* from the
merchants and the liberal *ulama* - renegade *ulama* often
appeared as local *Babi* leaders (cf. Avery 1965, pp.
52 f). But, all things considered, support for the
movement was very limited, and the sporadic armed
uprisings in Mazandaran, Zanjan, Yazd and Nayriz
were far from being a threat to the Qajar state.
European observers who regarded the movement with
sympathy (Gobineau and Browne) - and conversely had
a hostile attitute towards Islam - have undoubtedly
exaggerated the significance of the movement. Algar
1979, pp. 137-51 claims that the movement should to
some extent be seen as the result of a clash within
the *ulama* (but in general his interpretation of the
phenomenon accords ill with the broad lines in his
theory of the role of the *ulama*).

31) Both places were *bast*, i.e. sacrosanct. The efforts
of the Qajar state to reduce the number of these traditional sanctuaries and make it difficult for people
to escape arrest roused widespread opposition among
the *ulama*.

32) Cecil Spring Rice. The hostile tone in the description is presumably due to the fact that, like so many other Europeans, he despised Islam and regarded the *Babis* deadly enemies of the *ulama*, with sympathy.

33) In a few cases, however, it was considered safest to have it. During an uprising in 1810 against the *vazir* of Isfahan the rebels applied to the city's *Shaykh al-Islam* for a *fatva* endorsing the lynching, if necessary, of the agents of the *vazir* (Ouseley 1819 II, pp. 208 ff).

34) The extent of Russian interference in the agitation against the British concession is unknown (cf. Keddie 1966) nor is it crucial for the understanding of the course of the revolt.

35) The annulment also meant an economic burden, as the Shah had to pay the British concessionaires a considerable sum in compensation.

36) It is indicative of the attitude of the radical *ulama* today that they have rehabilitated Shaykh Fazl'ullah Nuri and other anti-*majlis ulama* who were branded by their contemporaries as reactionary minions of Muhammad Ali Shah. Now they are praised for their steadfast resistance to the insidious penetration of European norms (see for example G. Rose 1983, pp. 182 f).

Abbreviations:

EI/2   Encyclopedia of Islam, 2. ed.

IBZ   O. Hoetzsch (ed.): Die Internationalen Beziehungen im Zeitalter des Imperialismus, 1. Serie I-IX, Berlin 1931-32.

IJMES   International Journal of Middle East Studies.

IS   Iranian Studies.

JRGS   Journal of the Royal Geographical Society.

References:

Abbot, K.E.   : "Notes taken on a Journey eastwards
1857   from Shiraz to Fessa and Darab..."
                        JRGS 27, pp. 149-184.

Abrahamian, E.   : "The Crowd in Iranian Politics, 1905-
1968   1953." Past & Present 41, pp. 184-
                        210.

Abrahamian, E.   : "Oriental Despotism: The Case of
1974   Qajar Iran." IJMES 5, pp. 3-31.

Abrahamian, E.   : "The Causes of the Constitutional
1979   Revolution in Iran." IJMES 10, pp.
                        381-414.

Abrahamian, E.   : Iran between Two Revolutions. Prince-
1982   ton 1982.

Algar, H.   : Religion and State in Iran, 1785-1906:
1969   The Role of the Ulama in the Qajar
                        Period. Berkeley-Los Angeles 1969.

Algar, H.   : "The Oppositional Role of the Ulama
1972   in Twentieth-century Iran.". N.R.
                        Keddie (ed.) Scholars, Saints, and
                        Sufis. Berkeley-Los Angeles 1972,
                        pp. 231-55.

Algar, H.   : Shi'ism and Iran in the Eighteenth
1977   Century." T. Naff & R. Owen (eds.):
                        Studies in Eighteenth Century Islamic
                        History. Carbondale 1977, pp. 288-302.

Arjomand, S.A.   : "Religion and Ideology in the Consti-
1979   tutional Revolution." IS 12, pp. 283-91.

Arjomand, S.A.   : "The Ulama's Traditionalist Opposition
1981   to Parliamentarism: 1907-1909." Middle
                        Eastern Studies 17, pp. 174-90.

Ashraf, A.   : "Historical Obstacles to the Develop-
1970   ment of a Bourgeoisie in Iran.". M.A.
                        Cook (ed.): Studies in the Economic
                        History of the Middle East. London 1970.

Avery, P.W.   : Modern Iran. London 1965.
1965

Avery, P.W. &   : "Persia on a Cross of Silver, 1880-
Simmons J.B.   1890.". E. Kedourie & S.G. Haim (eds.):
1980   Towards a Modern Iran, London 1980,
                        pp. 1-37.

Aubin, E.
1908
: La Perse d'aujourd'hui. Paris 1908.

Bakhash, S.
1978
: Iran: Monarchy, Bureaucracy and Reform under the Qajars. London 1978.

Banani,
1978
: Reflections on the Social and Economic Structure of Safavid Persia. In: Iranian Studies, Vol. 11, 1978, pp. 83-116.

Bassett, J.
1887
: Persia. The Land of the Imams. London 1887.

Brockway, T.P.
1941
: "Britain and the Persian Bubble." Journal of Modern History 13, pp. 36-47.

Browne, E.G.
1910
: The Persian Revolution, 1905-1909. Cambridge 1910.

Bulliet, R.W.
1972
: The Patricians of Nishapur. Cambridge (Mass.) 1972, p. 20.

Busch, B.C.
1967
: Britain and The Persian Gulf, 1894-1914. Berkeley/Los Angeles 1967.

Busse, H.
1972
: "Kerman im 19. Jahrhundert nach der Geographie des Waziri." Der Islam 49, pp. 284-312.

Christensen, P.
1975
: Iran 1890-1914. Mimeographed MA-thesis. University of Copenhagen 1975.

Christensen, P.
1982
: "Et Bondesamfund i forfald? - Imperiedannelse og økologisk balance i Iran." Fortid og Nutid XXIX, 1982, pp. 607-625.

Curzon, G.N.
1892
Persia and the Persian Question I-II. London 1892.

Dunbuli, Abd'r-
Razzaq Bayg b. Nadjaf
Quli Khan Maftun.
: The Dynasty of the Kajars. Sir Harford Jones (trans.), London 1833.

Eastwick, E.B.
1864
: Three Years' Residence in Persia I-II. London 1864.

Eliash, J.
1969
: "The Ithna'ashari Shii Juristic Theory of Political and Legal Authority." Studia Islamica 29, pp. 17-30.

Eliash, J.
1979
: "Misconceptions Regarding the Juridical Status of the Iranian 'Ulama." IJMES 10, pp. 9-25.

English, P.W.   : City and Village in Iran. Settlement
1966   and Economy in the Kirman Basin.
                   Madison 1966.

Entner, M.L.   : Russo-Persian Commercial Relations,
1965   1828-1914. Gainesville (Univ. of
                   Florida Monographs. Social Sciences
                   28) 1965.

Fasa'i, H.   : History of Persia under Qájár Rule.
1972   Trans. H. Busse. New York 1972.

Fathi, A.   : "The Role of the "Rebels" in the Con-
1979   stitutional Movement in Iran."
                   IJMES 10, pp. 55-56.

Fathi, A.   : "The Role of the Traditional Leader
1980   in the Modernization of Iran, 1890-
                   1910." IJMES 11, pp. 87-98.

Feuvrier   : Trois ans á la Cour de Perse.
1895   Paris 1895.

Fischer, M.   : "Persian Society: Transformation and
1977   Strain." H. Amirsadeghi & R.W. Fer-
                   rier (eds.): Twentieth-Century Iran.
                   London 1977, pp. 171-195.

Floor, W.M.   : "The Office of Kalántar in Qájár Persia."
1971   Journal of the Economic and Social Hi-
                   story of the Orient 14, pp. 253-68.

Floor, W.M.   : "The Police in Qájár Persia."
1973   Zeitschrift d. Deutschen Morgenländ.
                   Gesellschaft 123, pp. 293-315.

Floor, W.M.   : "The Revolutionary Character of the
1980   Iranian Ulama: Wishful Thinking or
                   Reality?" IJMES 12, pp. 501-24.
                   Reprinted in N.R. Keddie (ed.): Reli-
                   gion and Politics in Iran, New Haven
                   1983, pp. 73-97.

Fraser, J.B.   : Narrative of a Journey into Khorasan.
1825   London 1825.

Fraser, J.B.   : Travels in Koordistan, Mesopotamia &
1840   I-II. London 1840.

Garthwaite, G.R. : "The Bakhtiyari Khans, The Govern-
1972   ment of Iran, and the British, 1846-
                   1915. IJMES 3, pp. 24-44.

Garthwaite, G.R. : "The Bakhtiyari Ilkhani: an Illusion
1977   of Unity." IJMES 8, pp. 145-160.

Garthwaite, G.R.   : "Pastoral Nomadism and Tribal Power."
1978   IS 11, pp. 173-97.

Goldsmid, F.J. (ed.)   : Eastern Persia, an Account of the
1876   Journeys of the Persian Boundary Com-
                            mission, Vol. I, London 1876.

Greaves, R.L.   : Persia and the Defence of India,
1959   1884-1892. London 1959.

Gwynn, S. (ed.)   : The Letters and Friendships of Sir
1929   Cecil Spring Rice. London 1929, I,
                            p. 296 f.

Hairi, A.-H.   : Shi'ism and Constitutionalism in Iran.
1977   Leiden 1977.

Hakluyt, R.   : Principal Navigations, Voyages, Traf-
1598-1600   fics and Discoveries of the English
                            Nation. London 1598-1600.

Hambly, G.R.G.   : "Aqa Mohammad Khan and the Establish-
1963   ment of the Qajar Dynasty."
                            Royal Central Asian Journal 50.

Hambly, G.R.G.   : "An Introduction to the Economic Orga-
1964   nization of Early Qajar Iran."
                            Iran II, pp. 69-81.

Hinz, W.   : "Shah Esma'il II." Mitteilungen des
1933   Seminars für Orientalische Sprachen
                            XXXVI, 1933, pp. 19-100.

Hurewitz, J.C. (ed.)   : Diplomacy in the Middle East.
1965   Princeton 1965, Vol. I, No. 35.

Inalcik, H.   : "The socio-political effects of the
1975   diffusion of fire-arms in the Middle
                            East." In: V.J. Parry & M.E. Yapp
                            (eds.): War, Technology and Society
                            in the Middle East. London 1975,
                            pp. 195-217.

Issawi, C.   : The Economic History of Iran, 1800-
1971   1914. Chicago 1971.

Kasravi, A.   : Táríkh-é Mashrúté-yé. Tihran 1350.
1350

Kazemi, F. &   : "The Nonrevolutionary Peasantry of
Abrahamian, E.   Modern Iran." IS 11, pp. 259-304.
1978

Kazemzadeh, F.   : Russia and Britain in Persia, 1964-
1968   1914. New Haven 1968.

Keddie, N.R.   : Religion and Rebellion in Iran:
1966 (a)   The Tobacco Protest of 1891-1892.
                            London 1966.

Keddie, N.R.   : "The Origins of the Religious-Radical
1966 (b)   Alliance in Iran." Past & Present 34,
                      pp. 70-80.

Keddie, N.R.   : "The Roots of the Ulama's Power in
1972   Modern Iran." N.R. Keddie (ed.):
                      Sufis, Saints, and Scholars.
                      Berkeley-Los Angeles 1972, pp. 213-29.

Keddie, N.R.   : "Class Structure and Political Power
1978   in Iran since 1796." IS 11, pp. 305-30.

Keddie, N.R.   : "Iran: Change in Islam; Islam and
1980   Change." IJMES 11, pp. 527-42.

Keddie, N.R.   : "Introduction", N.R. Keddie (ed.):
1983   Religion and Politics in Iran.
                      New Haven, pp. 1-18, 182 f.

Kinneir, J.   : A Geographical Memoir of the Persian
MacDonald   Empire. London 1813.
1813

Lambton, A.K.S.   : Landlord and Peasant in Persia.
1953   London 1953.

Lambton, A.K.S.   : "Secret Societies and the Persian
1958   Revolution of 1905-6." St Antony's
                      Papers 4/ Middle Eastern Affairs 1,
                      pp. 43-60.

Lambton, A.K.S.   : "Persian Society under the Qajars."
1961   Journal of the Royal Central Asian
                      Society 48, pp. 123-39.

Lambton, A.K.S.   : "Persian Political Societies 1906-11."
1963   St Antony's Papers 16/Middle Eastern
                      Affairs 3, pp. 41-89.

Lambton, A.K.S.   : "The Tobacco Regie: Prelude to Revo-
1965   lution." Studia Islamica 22-23, pp.
                      119-57, 71-90.

Lambton, A.K.S.   : "The Case of Hajji Nur al-Din, 1823-
1967   47: a Study in Land Tenure."
                      Bulletin of the School of Oriental
                      and African Studies 30, pp. 54-72.

Lambton, A.K.S.   : "Persian Trade under the Early Qajars."
1970 (a)   D.S. Richards (ed.): Islam and the
                      Trade of Asia. Oxford 1970, pp. 215-
                      44.

Lambton, A.K.S.   : "The Persian Ulama and Constitutional
1970 (b)   Reform." Le Shi'isme Imamite, Paris
                      1970, pp. 245-69.

Lambton, A.K.S.
1971

: "The Case of Hajji Abd al-Karim: a Study of the Role of the Merchant in mid-nineteenth-century Persia." C.E. Bosworth (ed.): Iran and Islam. Edinburgh 1971, pp. 331-360.

Lambton, A.K.S.
1974

: "Some New Trends in Islamic Political Thought in late 18th and early 19th century Persia." Studia Islamica 39, pp. 95-128.

Lambton, A.K.S.
1977

: "The Tribal Resurgence and the Decline of Bureaucracy in the Eighteenth Century." T. Naff & R. Owen (eds.): Studies in Eighteenth Century Islamic History. Carbondale 1977, pp. 108-29.

Layard, A.H.
1846

: "A Description of the Province of Khuzistan." JRGS 16, pp. 1-105.

Litten, W.
1920

: Persien: von der "Pénétration Pacifique" zum "Protektorat", 1860-1919. Berlin 1920.

Lockhart, L.
1959

: "The Persian Army in the Safavid Period." Der Islam 34, 1959, pp. 89-98.

MacGregor, C.M.
1879

: Narrative of a Journey through the Province of Khorassan I-II. London 1879.

McNeill, J.
1910

: Memoir of the Right Hon. Sir John McNeill and his Second Wife Elizabeth Wilson. London 1910.

Malcolm, J.
1828

: Sketches of Persia I-II. London 1828.

Malcolm, J.
1829

: History of Persia I-II. London 1829.

Masson Smith jr.,
1978

: "Turanian Nomadism and Iranian Politics." IS 11, pp. 57-81.

Minorsky, V.
(ed. & trans.)
1943

: Tadhkirat al-Muluk. A Manual of Safavid Administration. Cambridge 1943. E.J.W. Gibb Memorial New Series XVI.

Norris, J.A.
1967

: The First Afghan War, 1838-1842. Cambridge 1967.

O'Donnovan, E.
1882

: The Merv Oasis I-II. London 1882.

Ouseley, W.
1819
: Travels in Various Countries of the
East; more particularly Persia I-III.
London 1819-23.

Reid, J.J.
1978
: "The Qajar Uymaq in the Safavid Period, 1500-1722." IS 11, pp. 117-43.

Rose, G.
1983
: "Velayat-e-Faqih and the Recovery of
Islamic identity in the thought of
Ayatollah Khomeini." In: N.R. Keddie
(ed.): Religion and Politics in Iran.
New Haven 1983, pp. 182 f.

Röhrborn, K.-M.
1966
: Provinzen und Zentralgewalt Persiens
im 16. und 17. Jahrhundert. Berlin
1966.

Savory, R. M.
1964
: "Some notes on the provincial administration of the early Safavid Empire."
Bulletin of the School of Oriental
and African Studies XXVII 1964, pp.
114-128.

Sheikholeslami, A.R.
1978
: "The Patrimonial Structure of Iranian
Bureaucracy in the late Nineteenth
Century." IS 11, pp. 199-258.

Sheil, J.
1838
: "Notes on a Journey from Tabriz..."
JRGS 8, pp. 54-101.

Sheil, Lady
1856
: Glimpses of Life and Manners in Persia.
London 1856.

Spring Rice
1929
: S. Gwynn (ed.): The Letters and Friendships of Sir Cecil Spring Rice I-II.
London 1929.

Stewart, C.E.
1911
: Through Persia in Disguise. London
1911.

Sykes, P.M.
1902
: Ten Thousand Miles in Persia.
London 1902.

Tabari, A.
1983
: "The Role of the Clergy in Modern
Iranian Politics." N.R. Keddie (ed.):
Religion and Politics in Iran.
New Haven 1983, pp. 47-72.

Taqizadeh, H.
1960
: "The Background of the Constitutional
Movement in Azerbayjan."
Middle East Journal 14.

Tate, G.P.
1910
: Seistan. A Memoir on the History,
Topography, Ruins, and People of the
Country I-II. Calcutta 1910.

Thornton, A.P. 1954	: "British Policy in Persia, 1858– 1890." English Historical Review 69 (pp. 554-79) & 70 (pp. 55-71).
Upton, J.M. 1961	: History of Modern Iran. Cambridge, Mass. 1961.
Waring, E.S. 1807	: A Tour to Sheraz... London 1807.
Watson, R.G. 1866	: A History of Persia from the Begin- ning of the Nineteenth Century to the Year 1858. London 1866.
Wills, C.J. 1887	: Persia as it is. London 1887 (2. ed.).
Wills, C.J. 1891	: In the Land of the Lion and the Sun, or Modern Persia. London 1891 (new ed.).
Wolf, E.R. 1973	: Peasant Wars of the Twentieth Century. New York 1973.
Woods, J.E. 1976	: The Aqquyunlu. Clan, Confederation, Empire. Minneapolis 1976.
Yapp, M.E. 1977	: "1900-1921: The Last Years of the Qajar Dynasty." H. Amirsadeghi & R.W. Ferrier (eds.): Twentieth-Cen- tury Iran. London 1977, pp. 1-22.

THE POLITICAL USE OF ISLAM IN AFGHANISTAN
DURING THE REIGN OF AMIR ABDUR RAHMAN (1880-1901)

by

Asta Olesen

Introduction

The history of Afghanistan during the last one hundred and
fifty years clearly shows Islam to be an important political force. During the 19th century, Afghanistan's internal development and external political relations were
largely shaped by the country's location as a buffer state
between Tsarist Russia and British India. In all confrontations with the two Christian imperialist powers, Islam played an important role in mobilising popular resistance a-
gainst foreign encroachment.

     During the reign of Amir Abdur Rahman (1880-1901, Islam
was also skilfully and very forcefully put to internal use
in Afghanistan to prove the ideological legitimacy of the
Amir and of his policy of centralisation. The Amir had the
double aim of breaking the power of traditional power groups,
tribal leaders and the clergy and, at the same time,strength-
ening the position of Islam as the unifying factor of the
heterogeneous society. To a large extent this policy succeeded and, in a positive as well as a negative sense, formed the basis for the development of Afghan society during
the 20th century.

The relationship with British India and Tsarist Russia and its consequences

In the 19th century two themes dominated the situation in
Afghanistan - internal disorder and external pressures
from foreign invasions:

"The final dismemberment of the Durrani Empire
occurred. Punjab, Sind, Kashmir, and most of
Baluchistan was irrevocably lost, as the Mohammadzai (Barakzai) and Saddozai princes (both
Durrani Pushtuns) fought for regional control.
Within each region, father fought son, brother
fought brother, half brother fought half brother,
uncle fought nephew in a neverending round-robin
of blood-letting and blindings. They contested
for four major areas, Kabul, Qandahar, Herat, and
the northern Uzbak Khanates, usually either in-
dependently or in alliances to contest each other
for power."

(Dupree 1973, p. 343)

The external situation was characterised by the Russian expansion in Central Asia and the British expansion and consolidation on the Indian sub-continent. The very geo-
graphic location of Afghanistan as the gateway to India
brought it within the sphere of influence of both imperialist powers.

The Anglo-Afghan relationship began when Mountstuart
Elphinstone effected a pact with Afghanistan in 1809 (a
mutual defence treaty against Franco-Persian aggression)
in which the two governments pledged eternal friendship and
"in no manner to interfere in each other's country"
(Gregorian 1969, p. 94). The British, however, failed to
honour this pact and continued during the 19th century to
vacillate between a forward policy and a stationary policy.
The Russian advances in Asia (Treaty of Turkmanchai, 1828,
with Persia, and Treaty of Adrianople, 1829, with the Ottoman Empire) led the British to adopt the so-called forward
policy designed to secure British hegemony in Persia and
Afghanistan. Afghanistan was henceforth to be regarded as
the frontier of India and no European nation would be permitted to carry on commercial or political activities there,
or to interfere, directly or indirectly, in Afghan affairs
(Gregorian 1969, p. 96).

There was, however, no uniform agreement over the
Afghan policy in Britain. Proponents of the stationary
policy argued that a consolidation on the north-western
frontier of India along the Sutlej River would ensure for
Britain an effective government in India, would promote

trade, provide greater security, and enable a greater economic hold over India (Gregorian 1969, p. 96).

Direct British interference in internal Afghan politics
resulted the Anglo-Afghan War of 1839-42 where the attempt
to install the British puppet Shah Shuja in Kabul failed la-
mentably. In the following years a stationary policy prevailed which restricted British interference in Afghan affairs to more indirect means such as financial subsidies to
the Amir and a friendship treaty in 1857. The expediency
of this policy soon proved itself to the British, as it prevented the Afghans from lending support to the Sepoy Rebellion which was shaking the empire in 1857. In point of fact,
however, in the population at large religious animosity a-
gainst the foreigners was rapidly increasing, secretly exploited by the Peshawari Brothers, the half-brothers of the
Afghan Amir, Dost Muhammad (Tate 1911, p. 159). Continued
Russian advances in Central Asia and the risk of the Russians exploiting non-Pashtun areas of northern Afghanistan as
a foothold for an advance towards India eventually led the
British to return to the forward policy. The objectives of
the forward policy were to preclude Russian gains in Central Asia, to provide India with a scientific frontier and
to bring Afghanistan under tighter British supervision and
control.[1] The viceroy of India, Lord Lytton, expressed the
British attitude in Afghanistan very bluntly: "Afghanistan
is a state far too weak and barbarous to remain isolated
and wholly uninfluenced between two great military empires
....We cannot allow Sher Ali to fall under the influence
of any power whose interests are antagonistic to our own."
(Gregorian 1969, pp. 111-112).

When the Russians despatched a diplomatic mission to
Kabul (1878, General Stolietov) seeking a mutual assistance
treaty with Afghanistan, the British saw the alternatives
to be either a negotiated diplomatic settlement with the
Afghan Amir that would permanently ensure British influence in Afghanistan, or, failing that, the destruction of
the Afghan kingdom and the conquest of as much Afghan territory as was necessary to secure the Indian frontier.

Diplomacy failed and the outcome was the second Afghan War in 1879. This was concluded with the Treaty of Gandamak by which it was agreed that Afghan foreign policy should be controlled by the British, that English representatives should be stationed in Kabul and in other strategic places and that there should be an extension of British control in the northwest frontier region. In return, the Amir was to receive £60,000 per annum (Dupree 1973, p. 409).

In the end, however, the objectives of the forward policy were not achieved. With the return of the Liberals to power in England, the view predominated that a total dismemberment of Afghanistan might well weaken the Indian frontier and threaten the British presence in the Panjab.

Influenced by these considerations, a new British administration in India under Lord Ripon took a bold step to achieve a political settlement of the Afghanistan question by recognising the candidacy of Abdur Rahman to the throne of Kabul. This was a particularly daring move since Abdur Rahman had spent some eleven years of exile in Russia after his involvement in internal warfare over the succession and had presumably returned to Afghanistan with the approval of the Tsarist government, perhaps even with its financial assistance (Gregorian 1969, p. 117).

The political development in Afghanistan and the whole social order in the country were greatly affected by its position as a buffer state between the two imperialist powers. Besides suffering two major wars, foreign occupation and annexation of territory, the economy was dislocated, the urban sector almost completely in ruins[2] while the power of the religious leaders increased and tribal leaders consolidated their position vis-à-vis the central state.

While the Afghan State had successfully used repression to deal with either internal disturbances or external threats, the combination of both almost caused a breakdown of central power in the country. From this time onward, the struggle against foreign invaders was led by traditional power groups

in the country, tribal leaders and the religious establishment, with whose enhanced power and prestige the rulers
thereafter had to reckon (Ghani 1977, p. 4).

Tribes and the Central State

With the distintegration and (consequent power vacuum in
the area) of the Safavid and Moghul empire, Afghanistan appeared in 1747 as an independent tribal kingdom. The label
tribal kingdom implies the sort of problems which the central
power was facing. In dealing with the Afghan (Pashtun)
tribes, which formed the military and political backbone of
the kingdom, the Afghan monarchs were subject to the same
limitations of authority as the tribal chieftains of those
basically egalitarian tribes. The actions and decisions of
the rulers had to conform to *pashtunwali* (the Pashtun tribal
code), to the *sharia* and especially to the decisions of the
jirga (tribal councils), which were based on the concept of
communal authority. A distinctive feature of Afghan tribal-
ism was that the real instrument of social control was the
pashtunwali and *jirga*, rather than the position of chieftain-
cy. With its democratic spirit and tenets, the *jirga* defied
political centralisation, and its constant accomodation of
regional interests made it a particularly divisive force in
the drive to form a modern and unified state (Gregorian 1969,
pp. 40-41). *Pashtunwali* , which set the limits of acceptable
behaviour within the community and governed the relations
between tribes[3] equally counteracted attempts at the centralisation of political power and legal and economic en-
croachments. *Rawaj* (customary law) varied from tribe to
tribe and from region to region - in general it instituti-
onalised local socio-economic interests. It often not only
circumvented the laws of the kingdom but also modified the
tenets of Islam. Politically, the tenuous authority structure made the tribes volatile and difficult to control or
direct for any sustained period along any given course of
action. Leadership was much more dependent on the personal
qualities of the leader than on obedience or loyalty to a

hierarchy. The ruler was viewed by the tribes merely as a
superior chief, a power or a man of personal qualities ad-
mired by the tribes (Poullada 1970; see also Bellew 1962,
pp. 121-122). The ongoing tribal rivalries and feuds among
the Pashtun tribes[4] could be manipulated by the rulers to
consolidate the central power. And the existence of a central power also influenced the social structure of the
tribes by strengthening the authority and power of the
chieftains politically and economically, for example through
land grants and taxation rights. The patrimonial commune
system was disintegrating and gradually being replaced by a
spiritual aristocracy (Gregorian 1969, pp. 42-43). However,
this feudalisation process took place at a very uneven rate
among the Pashtun tribes and was most pronounced among
those closest to the seat of central power (i.e., the Durranis) (see Oesterdiekhoff 1978).

These developments did not necessarily ease the task
of the Afghan rulers in the matter of centralisation and
unification. From the outset the budding Afghan State had
to contend with tribal chieftains and feudal lords bent on
preserving their privileged positions. By definition the
Afghan king was the hereditary chief and military commander
of the Durrani tribe; nevertheless he was bound by the will
of the Durrani *sardars* (leaders of royal lineage) since his
rule depended on their good will and military strength
(Gregorian 1969, p. 46). With no formalised rule of succession, the struggle for power among the Durrani *sardars*,
which involved patricide, fratricide and other atrocities,
easily matched and became related to tribal feuds and rivalries in the country as a whole. The centralising policies
of the rulers between 1747-1880 were in general impeded by
four factors - the tribal leaders, the royal lineage, the
religious establishment and the foreign powers. With the
latter weakening the Afghan State, the former groups grew
stronger vis-à-vis the state. Thus this period displays a
constancy of conflict between the rulers and the religious
establishment, the latter maintaining the usual alliance

65

with the tribel leadership, (Ghani 1978, p. 270).

While the central power, politically and militarily, originated from, and was based upon, the Pashtun tribes, it had not yet been able to supersede the structural limitations of the tribal state with its inherent disintegrating effects. The constant state of tension and uneasy power balance between the tribes and the central state is contained in the saying that the tribes in Afghanistan were both "king-makers and breakers" (Poullada 1970, p. 23). On the politico-ideological level this situation presented itself in the problem of the legitimacy of the state, where a dichotomous situation existed:

DICHOTOMY IN THE LEGITIMATION OF THE TRANSMISSION OF POWER[4a]

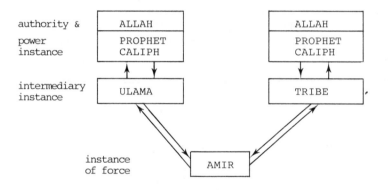

In a Muslim society, the legitimacy of power and of the ruler is ultimately derived from Allah and the Prophet, with the *ulama* as the intermediary. However, in Afghanistan at that time, this model of legitimacy was not generally accepted, since Islam as adhered to by the tribesmen did not have the *Sharia* as its judicial basis (in the case of differences, the *Sharia* was normally superseded by *pashtunwali*) and no local religious tradition enforced allegiance to monarchs (Ghani 1978, p. 269). Rather, legitimacy of power,

although ultimately deriving from Allah, was mediated through
the tribe(s), and consequently became closely involved with
pashtunwali and the concepts of equality and communal authority of the *jirga* (i.e. a tribal-state model of legitimacy).
For the Pashtun, the putative genealogical links to the
Prophet through the apical ancestor Qais made this model
and the bypassing of the religious establishment acceptable and compatible with Islam, since Muslim identity was
inherent in being Pashtun (Ahmed 1980, pp. 106-107). However, in the constant balance of power between the tribes
and the rulers, the latter increasingly attempted to claim
legitimacy on the basis of the "Islamic model", by appealing
to a source of legitimacy external to the tribal system.
This became particularly pronounced during the varied confrontations with the imperialist Christan powers, where,
for example, Amir Dost Muhammad declared himself as *Amir
al-muminin*[5] (commander of the faithful), and Amir Sher Ali
claimed divine sanction of his rule. Eventually a confron-
tation between these two models of legitimacy could not be
avoided in the sphere of practical politics, and under the
reign of Amir Abdur Rahman (as will be seen) this situation
became acute.

The Religious Situation in Afghanistan

> "...every priest, mullah, and chief of every
> tribe and village considered himself an in-
> dependent king, and for about 200 years past
> the freedom and independence of many of these
> priests were never broken by their sovereigns."
>
> (Mahomed 1900, I, p. 217)

The above evaluation of the clergy's power in Afghanistan
up to 1880 by Amir Abdur Rahman was not unfounded. From
the time of the Durrani kingdom and to the reign of Abdur
Rahman, the religious establishment enjoyed economic self-
sufficiency through direct land-ownership or control of religious endowments (*auqaf*) and through religious taxes. In
1815, Elphinstone described how many *mullas* lent money on
compounded interest (something which is prohibited as *sud*

in the Quran) by which they had greatly multiplied their
wealth and had acquired a considerable share of the landed
property of the kingdom. Others had achieved ecclesiastic-
al office[6] or pensions from the crown, and many had land
grants from the king or from village headmen, and some had
received legacies of land from individuals. Many groups of
village *imams* received a certain share of the harvest or
from the flocks in their districts. Others lived by teaching and practising law, or as school teachers or tutours to
the sons of rich men, while some lived from charitable allowances granted by the crown and donated by the population
(Elphinstone 1839 I, pp. 285-286).

The religious establishment was in charge of learning,
education, the interpretation of the *sharia*, the administration of justice and the supervision (enforcement) of public
morals through the office of the *muhtasib*.[7] In addition,
Muslim clerics often acted as intermediaries or served as
peacemakers among warring tribes, which further increased
their social and political power (Gregorian 1969; Elphin-
shone 1839 I, Chapters II & V).

> "...and these advantages, together with the re-
> spect which their superior knowledge commands
> among an ignorant and superstitious people, en-
> able the moollahs in some circumstances to excer-
> cise an almost unlimited power over individuals,
> and even bodies of men; to check and control the
> governors and other civil officers; and sometimes
> to intimidate and endanger the King himself. This
> power is employed to punish practices contrary to
> the Mohammedan law...; to repress Sheeahs and
> other infidels; and, at least as often, to revenge
> the wrongs or forward the interests of individuals
> of the religious order."
>
> (Elphinstone 1839 I, p. 282)

The rulers were thus faced with two important power groups
in the country - the tribal leaders and the religious
leaders who, because of their religious knowledge and
actual power in the administration of justice, had a very
big influence on the population. Hence, the rulers were
careful not to antagonise the religious establishment and
paid them regular allowances (*wazifas*) (Kakar 1971, pp.4-5).

In fact, half the revenue of the whole kingdom was spent in allowances to the *mullas*,*sayyids*, *pirs* and others of religious calling (Mohamed 1900 I, p. 252).[8]

Although the religious leaders were able to exert considerable influence at the national level, it was not until 1931 (during the reign of Nader Shah) when *Jamiyyat-i-ulama* was founded, that the religious establishment obtained a formal corporate body to represent their interests and view at a national level. Until then, *ulamas* had existed at the regional level only in such centres as Kabul, Kandahar and Herat. The education of the *mullas* was, until the reign of Amir Abdur Rahman, quite diversified, many being educated abroad, in India, Bukhara, Tashkent and Samarkand (Sirat 1969, p. 219). The biggest religious differences in Afghanistan existed between the *sunni* and the minority *shia* groups; the latter were mainly made up of the Hazaras of the central highland and the influential Qizilbash community in Kabul. But even within the majority *sunni* group, there was no uniformity of religious belief and practice.

Islam as practised by the Pashtun tribes was radically different from that advocated by the *ulama*. While the identification as Muslims was clear, observance of the legal injunctions of the *sharia* was almost non-existent. Some tribesmen were also lax in observing the fast and daily prayers (Ghani 1977, p. 23). In Bellew's formulation this situation appears at best a paradox, and at worst hyprocrisy:

> "The Afghans are very proud of their devotion to
> Islam - and affect scrupulous adherence to its
> principles. But they do not by their conduct
> maintain either the credit of the religion they
> profess or their own character for sincerity;
> for though they punish the blasphemer and
> apostate by stoning to death - they do not
> scruple to depart from or set in direct opposi-
> tion to the most binding or important of their
> religious laws, when by so doing they can attain
> the object of their desires without personal
> risk or detriment to their interests."

(Bellew 1862, pp. 27-28)

The explanation seems to lie in the Pashtuns' concept of
the relationship between *pashtunwali* and Islam. As mentioned earlier, the rules of behaviour and justice for the
Pashtun is derived from three sources: *Pashtunwali, rawaj*
(customary law), and Islam, where Islam is not the most
prominent. However, this does not indicate a conflict or
a contradiction between Islam and *pashtunwali*; on the contrary; for the Pashtun, Islam and *pashtunwali* support each
other: "Paradise in Islam is acquired through Pashtu...the
countless graces of Paradise come through Pashtu to the
Pashtuns" (Ghani 1977, p. 23). The Pashtun belief lies in
the history of conversion to Islam, by the Prophet himself,
of Qais bin Rashid (the common Pashtun ancestor), and the
patrilineal descent from him places religion as a defining
factor in Pashtun identity alongside *pashtunwali*. Obedience
and submission, total loyalty of his will to the infinite
power of the Almighty - that is all that is required of the
Pashtun and that is what he gives willingly. He is by definition a Muslim just as by birth he obtains inalienable
right to Pashtunness. His place in society as a Pashtun
and a Muslim is thus secure and defined from the moment of
birth; hence, Pashtunness and Muslimness do not have to
coalesce; they are within each other and the interiority of
the former is assumed in the latter (Ahmed 1980, p. 115).

Religious devotion in the form of saint cults (*pirs*)
were widespread, although the importance given to religious
dignitaries varied from tribe to tribe and from region to
region (see for example Spain, 1963). People of religious
knowledge or those who claimed holy descent (*sayyids,
khwajas*, etc.)[9] normally occupied a neutral position in
the tribal society, and this fact, together with their
superior knowledge, made them well-suited to the role of
mediator in conflicts, where they referred equally to
tribal law and to religious law. While the ordinary village *mulla* normally did not hold a very high position in
society, a person of religious renown could, through skilful use of his spiritual and political potential, achieve

and exercise considerable influence, particularly in time
of crisis, when these particular gifts were greatly needed.

The *sunni* population of the country thus did not ad-
here to a unified set of beliefs and practices, but rather
displayed considerable local differences, subscribed to
local or tribal customs, and were followers of local religious leaders, be it local *pirs* or organised *Sufi* Orders.[10]
The non-tribal part of the population, such as the Tajiks,
were not faced with the same problem of combining a tribal
code with Islam, but here also Islam as practised was mixed
with a lot of local non-Islamic beliefs and customs. The
cult of local saints was as frequent here as among the
tribes. Thus the picture of religious practices among the
sunni population was one of diversity and lack of unification.

The other big religious group (c. 14 per cent) in the
country was the *shias* – mainly consisting of the Hazara
population of the central Afghanistan and the influential
Qizilbash of Kabul. Ever since the formation of the Durrani
empire, the Hazaras had been subject to encroachment into
their territory, which forced them away from some of the
most fertile lands and into the central highlands.[11] It
was the policy of the rulers of Kabul to avoid an alliance
between the Qizilbash and the Hazaras since this was seen
as a threat to the State.[12] In principle, the *shia* faith
is more unified and hierarchical than sunnism. Religious
dignitaries among the *shias* enjoyed extremely high prestige
and influence because they either claimed descent from the
Prophet (were *sayyids*)[13] and/or because of their reputation for learning or pilgrimage to holy shrines especially
the *shia* shrines of Mashhad, Najaf and Kerbala.

However, the higher degree of hierarchisation of Hazara
society, where local clan chiefs and religious leaders of
sayyid descent exercised much more power than in the more
egalitarian Pashtun society, did not necessarily mean a
higher degree of internal unity. The clans and lineages
were not united into a unified tribal organisation, and

followers of the *sunni, shia* and *imami* faiths could be found within the one clan. Hence Hazara society was seen as internally conflict-ridden.[14]

At the national level, the power and influence of the religious leaders were drastically increased during the 19th century. The reasons were basically the weakening of the central power (which strengthened the two power groups, tribal elders and big landowners on the one side and the religious leaders on the other) and the continued attempts of foreign, Christian, intervention and aggression in Afghanistan. The rulers, with little military might of their own, had to mobilise the active military support of the tribes and other sections of the population in order to resist foreign aggression, and since neither the ruler nor the central power as such enjoyed general legitimacy in this very heterogeneous society, Islam appeared as the basic unifying force. In addition, Islam brought with it the concept of *jihad*, which put the believer against the infidel and implied a religious duty (*farz*) which carried a blessing in itself, in the titles, either as *ghazi* or as *shahid*.[15]

The word *jihad* generally refers to actual fighting. However, the word in itself has a much wider semantic content, as it can refer to exerting oneself for some praiseworthy aim (Peters 1979, Chapter 4).[16] *Jihad* in the sense of fighting is restricted by the phrase, *fi sabil Allah* (in the Way of Allah) which implies that *jihad* is not just ordinary war, but must be somewhat connected with religion and the interests of the believers. And *jihad* is not just the fighting itself, but everything that is conducive to victory.

One theory of *jihad* that developed in modern Islam concentrates upon the causes of warfare waged by the Muslims, and these fall in two categories - those connected with the propagation of Islam and those connected with the idea of defence. The causes connected with the latter concern:
(1) Repelling aggression on Muslim lives and property in case of an actual or expected attack by enemy forces. This

is founded on the following Sura from the Quran (2:190),
"Fight in the Way of Allah those who fight you, but do not
provoke hostility." (2) Preventing oppression and persecution of Muslims outside the Territory of Islam.[17] (3) Re-
taliating against a break of pledge by the enemy. This is
supported by the following Sura (9:21), "But if they
violate their oaths after they have made a covenant and
attack your religion, fight the leaders of unbelief; no
oath will hold in their case; mayhap they will refrain."

The Muslim world at the time of colonial expansion experienced a politicisation of Islam as the unifying ideology which should motivate Muslims to join hands in the anti-
colonial struggle. This view often found its expression in
pan-Islamism, of which Sayyid Jamal-ud-Din al-Afghani and
Abduh were prominent exponents. Colonial expansion was explained by pointing to the weakness inherent in Muslim societies, which had given the European powers a chance to
intrude into the Islamic world. The ultimate weakness
was, according to these movements, religious laxity and
decay and the abandonment of the principles of Islam. Hence,
the solution to the problems were clear and simple: the
purification of Islam by returning to its original principles and purging it of un-Islamic innovations and cor-
ruptions. The monotheistic character of islam was stressed and all kinds of polytheism (*shirk*) and unbelief (*kufr*)
condemned (Peters 1979, p. 153).

Jamal-ud-Din al-Afghani travelled throughout the Muslim
world spreading his pan-Islamic ideas. When he reached
Afghanistan from Persia in 1866-68 he appears to have exercised an anti-British influence on Amir Azam Khan and to
have urged closer ties with Russia as a counterweight to
the British. But when Sher Ali resumed power in Kabul,
Jamal-ud-Din al-Afghani failed to influence him against
the British since the latter were already giving him financial and military aid, and later al-Afghani was expelled by
the Amir (Keddie 1972, pp. 42-49). al-Afghani did not have
a very high opinion of the Afghans, as he believed the *ulama*

to be more harmful than useful since they labelled as *kafir*
anyone who did not agree with them. In 1879, however, when
it was important to stress to other Muslims the courage
with which the Afghans had stood up to the British in the
second Anglo-Afghan War, he painted quite another picture
(Keddie 1972, p. 55).

The encounter with the Christian imperialist powers
left a decisive mark on the ideological climate in Afghanistan. Until the first Anglo-Afghan War the attitude towards Europe was not an antagonistic one. Although the
country's educational establishment was governed by rigid
scholasticism and formalism, there seems to have been no
official antagonism, religious or secular, to Europeans
(see Elphinstone 1839). After the first Anglo-Afghan War,
when an upsurge of religious and national anti-British
feeling ended the rule of Shah Shuja, the attitude of the
Afghans changed dramatically. All Europeans were mistrusted; the English, and later the Russians, were looked on not
only as infidels but as enimies who threatened Afghan independence. The second Anglo-Afghan War deepened this reli-
gio-political antagonism. The off-and-on conflicts between
the frontier tribes and the British authorities in India,
and the general political conditions following the war,
sustained it (Gregorian 1969, pp. 118-123).

Through these wars, Islam served as a unifying national
force, but because of the weakened position of the urban
sectors, the nationalist, anti-British struggle was led primarily by the Afghan tribes and the religious establishment.
While the political application of Islam on the one hand
contributed greatly to the maintenance of Afghan independence, on the other hand the religious character of the struggle
and of the leadership promoted conservatism, Afghan xeno-
phobia and cultural isolationism. Many of the religious
leaders resisted the introduction and adoption of major socio-
economic and cultural innovations, despising them as alien
to the spirit and tenets of Afghan traditions. Most of them
identified such innovations with the Christian enemy, so the

rejection of European imperialism included rejection of
European civilisation as such (Gregorian 1969, pp. 126-
127).[18]

While the concept of *jihad* treated unity against the
foreigners, even across *sunni-shia* barriers, it did not
create internal unity. Within the Islamic concept of the
legitimacy of political power, a ruler is dependent upon the
Will of Allah. A muslim ruler, whether he be a Caliph, Amir,
King or President, rules with the divine sanction of Allah,
not with the divine right which has justified European
monarchies for centuries. If a Muslim ruler violates Islam
or goes against the Will of Allah, the sanction can thus be
removed (Dupree 1973, p. 465) and it becomes a religious
duty to choose a just Muslim rule: "These are they who have
bartered the guidance for error; their trade has not turned
out profitable and they have not been rightly guided
(*Sura* 2:16). "Upon them is the curse of Allah, and the
angles, and the people as a whole" (*Sura* 3:87). Thus was the
concept of *jihad* put to internal use in the endemic power
and succession struggles from which Afghanistan suffered
during the 19th century. Any contender to the throne would
seek to obtain a *fatva*[19] denouncing his opponent as an
apostate of Islam, perhaps because of alleged cooperation
with non-Muslims, an offence which would justify a *jihad*
against him. In this way, even the most secular of power
conflicts was given a religious cloak and Islam was manipulated to increase divisions in an already divided society.

Religion, Ideology and Politics

> "Islam is both a religion and state...It is to
> the credit of Islam that it has regulated re-
> ligious as well as worldly affairs. It deals
> not only with the relations between the Creator
> and the created, but also with the relations
> between man and man."
>
> (Muslehuddin 1977, pp.134-135)

Statements like this, where the theological-political character of Islam is clear, should not lead the non-Muslim

observer to reduce Islam to a merely political force, nor
can the political content of Islam be deduced from the
postulated eternal "essence" of this religion. On the contrary, in the words of Rodinson (1979, p. 12)

> "...religious ideologies, like all ideologies,
> have a concrete and real basis in the constantly
> competing human groups who share out the planet
> between themselves or form different strata of
> society. We can take into account the constant
> interaction of these groups and the fact that
> their primary consideration must be the demands
> of material and social life."

It should also be underlined that, while we are here concerned with the political use of Islam in a certain period
of Afghan society, this is but a single aspect and must be
conceptually distinguished from Islam as theology or Islam
as a religious experience or a way of life. Like most
religions, Islam must be considered at two distinct levels:
first, at the level of a universal philosophy, and second,
in its active form (including the various versions of local
Islam), whereby it is carried into the daily lives of the
masses by the interpretations of religious leaders, both
traditionalists and modernists (Dupree 1967, p. 198). Here
it must be noted that Islam, like any other religion or
dogma, is open to various and varied interpretations, which
in terms of political action can be called the operation-
alisation of the concept of Islamic polity. These interpretations differ greatly, depending upon the political and
social contexts and the historical point in time at which
they are brought into operation. They also vary in accordance with the particular medium through which such opera-
tionalisation takes place (Ayoob 1979, pp. 535-36). However, it is the existence of Islam as an implicit ideology
in society, consisting of local and popular interpretations
(often quite different from the explicit theological dogmas
of the *ulama*), and of Islamic culture in its widest sense,
which is an absolute precondition for the successful ope-
rationalisation of the concept of Islamic polity. The
concrete political use of Islam depends upon the creation

of a synthesis with the implicit ideology current in society
or among the social group addressed; anything significantly
running counter to this implicit ideology is bound to be rejected. In order to clarify this point, we must turn to
the concept of ideology itself. Ideology is normally very
loosely understood as "a set of ideas, beliefs, and ways of
thinking characteristic of a group such as a nation, a class,
a caste, a profession, a sect, or a political party."[20]
Following Laclau[21] the basic function of all ideology is
to transform/constitute individuals who are simple bearers
of structures into subjects through the mechanism of interpellation. Hence the unity of the distinct aspect of an
ideological system is given by the specific interpellation
which forms the axis and organising principle of all ideology (Laclau 1977, p. 101). Ideological elements, be they
religious, national or other elements, taken in isolation
have no necessary class connotation, and the class connotation is only the result of the articulation of those elements in a concrete ideological discourse. This means that
the precondition for analysing the class nature of an ideology is to conduct an inquiry through that which constitutes
the distinctive unity of an ideological discourse, i.e.,
the interpellative structure.

Through these theoretical clarifications it is clear
why the political (class) content of Islam cannot be a pri-
ori determined. Religious elements, national, popular-
democratic, and so on, can be integrative elements in widely different discourses. The political nature of an ideological discourse is not determined from the constituent
elements but from the structure of the interpellation. This
position requires further explanation and Laclau proceeds
to determine the field of ideological class struggle:
first, classes exist at the ideological and political level
in a process of articulation and not of reduction. This
means that not all contradictions are class contradictions,
but only those that constitute classes as such;[22] second,
articulation therefore requires the existence of non-class

contents - interpellations and contradictions - which constitute the raw material on which class ideological practices operate.

Rodinson touches upon the articulation of religious
elements with secular political ideologies:

> "I do not think that Islam is an autonomous po-
> litical ideology at present. The Muslim faith-
> ful are often enough apolitical, whether their
> faith encourages them in such an attitude or not.
> But the options in question can in no way be ex-
> plained in terms of the religious dogma. They
> remain aspects of these essentially secular ideo-
> logies...and simply provide these secular ideo-
> logies with a religious garb and a religious
> justification."

(Rodinson 1979, p. 199).

Rodinson here reduces the religious elements in secular
ideologies to a mere justification or manipulation. While
this situation might occur, it still neglects the fact
that for any (class) ideology to acquire hegemonic position in society, it is necessary that it should include and
articulate a wide range of popular-democratic, religious
and other ideological elements included in what earlier
was referred to as the implicit ideology of society.[23)]

In Afghanistan during the last century, there was no
economic, political or ideological unity nor homogeneity,
and the central state was but little developed. At the
ideological level Islam was the only unifying force and,
as pointed out, even the religious practices and beliefs
were highly diversified at the local level and coexisted
with tribal ideological models. The unstable character of
the central state was at the ideological level reflected
in the before-mentioned conflict between the Islamic and
tribal models of the legitimacy of power. This lack of
economic, political and ideological cohesion in Afghanistan was shared by many countries in the Third World where
the capitalist relations of production were not yet dominant and where the geographical boundaries are more or
less arbitrarily determined. In such a situation the

function of the state and ruling group is not to maintain
the ideological hegemony, but rather to create it. In
Afghanistan, Amir Abdur Rahman, more than anyone else, de-
voted his life to this task. Through a forceful and skilful use of Islamic concepts he aimed at establishing one
particular interpretation of Islam as the dominant and
state-supporting ideology of the country.

Amir Abdur Rahman Period[24]

When Abdur Rahman Khan resumed power in 1880, the task before him was, in his own words,

> "...to put in order all those hundreds of petty
> chiefs, plunderers, robbers, and cut-throats...
> This necessitated breaking down the feudal and
> tribal system and substituting one grand commu-
> nity under one law and one ruler."
>
> (Quoted from Wilber 1962, p. 19)

Abdur Rahman aimed at extending the authority of the Afghan
state into hitherto independent regions (like Kafiristan
and Hazarajat) and imposing taxation and rigid administration upon the rest of the country as a necessary means to
developing a centralised state. The ruthless execution of
this policy brought about more than forty internal disturbances during the reign of the "Iron Amir".[25] Included in
the above-mentioned political goals of the Amir was the consolidation of the royal lineage, i.e. the perpetuation of
the lineage's hegemony[26] under the overlordship of his
house within the frame of a centralised state. The rea-
lisation of this was dependent on the complete subordina-
tion of the lineage to the authority of the Amir (Ghani
1977, p. 119). Consequently, in the beginning of his reign,
Amir Abdur Rahman had to face considerable dynastic rivalries, particularly from his two cousins, Sardar Ayub (son
of Amir Sher Ali) and Sardar Muhammad Ishaq (son of Amir
Muhammad Azam Khan), who, being sons of former *amirs* had as
legitimate claims to the throne as Abdur Rahman (son of
Amir Muhammad Afzal) and enjoyed considerable popular support. Sardar Ayub had the support of the Durranis while

Ishaq was a popular and almost autonomous governor of Turkestan until 1888, where he staged a formidable revolt of
Ghilzai, Uzbeks and Turcomans against Amir Abdur Rahman,
but ultimately had to escape to Bukhara.

The unification and centralisation of Afghanistan was
carried out through administrative and economic measures
supported by a considerable strengthening of the executive
power, i.e. the army and the police forces.[27]

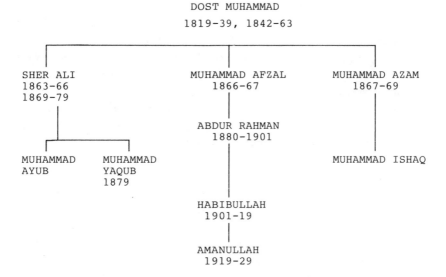

```
                       DOST MUHAMMAD
                     1819-39, 1842-63


 SHER ALI              MUHAMMAD AFZAL         MUHAMMAD AZAM
 1863-66                 1866-67               1867-69
 1869-79

                       ABDUR RAHMAN
                        1880-1901

 MUHAMMAD   MUHAMMAD                         MUHAMMAD ISHAQ
 AYUB       YAQUB
            1879

                       HABIBULLAH
                        1901-19

                       AMANULLAH
                        1919-29
```

Amir Abdur Rahman attempted to break the power of the tribal
leaders and to a considerable extent succeeded. The state
became the guarantor of law and order: no internal dispute
settlement was allowed in the tribe; every matter had to be
dealt with in a formal court where the *sharia* was made the
only binding law and *pashtunwali* was actively suppressed.[28]
An extensive secret police ensured that those regulations
were obeyed. The division into provinces criss-crossing the
tribal regions supported this development, and while the
provincial governors' powers vis-à-vis the tribes grew, they
remained under tight control from Kabul (Kakar 1979, Chapter 3).

Economic policy was basically a matter of imposing and, in particular, collecting new taxes.[29] Even the lands of tribal chiefs were subject to taxation and their right to levy duties on caravans was removed. In this way the independent economic power of the tribal chiefs was to some extent curtailed, while the Amir gave allowances to them depending upon the size of the tribe and the service which the chief could render to the government. Apart from the chief, most men of influence in the tribes received allowances from the state (Ghani 1977, pp. 102-104).

In general the power of the tribal leaders became largely dependent upon their good relationship with the Amir, who also managed to utilise factional conflicts and old enmities in a skilful divide-and-rule policy. A case in point is the Hazara Wars, where the Amir had great success in exploiting *sunni-shia* conflicts to recruit volunteers to fight the Hazaras. The Amir generally aimed at establishing a faction within the tribe loyal to himself by bestowing favours and through numerous marriage alliances (Mahomed 1900, II, p. 11). The tribes and chiefs who did not submit voluntarily to this sort of coercion were met with military force. Such campaigns as those against the powerful Ghilzai (late 1880's to early 1890's) were followed up by forced migrations of some 10,000 Ghilzai families to the north. This policy served two purposes - to remove the most rebellious people from their home region, and to make use of them as a loyal (Pashtun) force in alien (non-Pashtun) areas.[30]

Two of the most conspicuous campaigns of the Amir were against Hazarajat (1891-1893) and Kafiristan (1895-96), as both of these areas so far had been outside the control of the Afghan State and were populated by ethnic groups of different religious persuasion (the Hazaras adhering to *shia* Islam while the Kafirs were non-Muslims.[31] In the campaigns against the Hazaras, the Amir at first tried to exploit internal rivalries and, through coercion, imposed the suzerainty of the state upon these areas. However, when that form of suppression ultimately brought about a unity among the

Hazaras *against* the Afghan State, the Amir declared *jihad* against the Hazaras, recruited volunteers in the rest of the country by promising loot and slaves in return (Ghani 1977) and ultimately defeated the Hazaras.

By the end of Amir Abdur Rahman's rule, the power structure of Afghanistan was changed for good. Although the country as yet could hardly be called a unified, centralised state, the power of the tribes had been broken, and the state was now established as a centre of authority and power independent of the tribes and the tribal chiefs.

Relationships between the Clergy and the State

> "Many of these priests taught as Islamic religion strange doctrines which were never in the teaching of Mohamed, yet which have been the cause of the downfall of all Islamic nations in every country. They taught that people were never to do any work, but only to live on the property of others, and to fight against each other. Of course it is natural that every one of these self-made kings should have levied separate taxes on their subjects: so the first thing I had to do was to put an end to these numberless robbers, thieves, false prophets, and trumpery kings. I must confess that it was not a very easy task, and it took fifteen years of fighting before they finally submitted to my rule or left the country, either by being exiled or by departing into the next world."
>
> (Mohamed 1900, Vol. I, p. 218)

The Amir's above statement from Abdur Rahman's autobiography suggests, the Amir's relationship with the clergy was strained, and this was the case right from the beginning of his rule, when the *ulama* of Qandahar supported Sardar Ayub's claim to the throne by issuing a *fatva* denouncing Abdur Rahman as a "nominee of the British" and urging the people to rise against him in a *jihad*. After defeating Ayub, the Amir allowed two of the most prominent dignitaries, Mulla Abdul Rahim and Mulla Abdul Ahmad Akhundzada, who had signed the *fatva*, to be executed. However, Abdur Rahman did not himself refrain from making political use of religion and religious dignitaries: in Maidan he secured the

allegiance of 400 *mullas* and a *fatva* to denounce Ayub as a
'rebel'. (Kakar 1971, pp. 76-79).

Abdur Rahman's controversies with the religious leaders
were closely linked with his campaigns to break tribal resistance against centralisation. In most of the uprisings,
local or regional, religious dignitaries played an important role as they sanctioned the rebellion by delcaring that
the Amir was violating the interests of Islam or was an
outright *kafir*. In several instances, the leadership of a
rebellion consisted of a combination of tribal and religious
dignitaries; both were needed - the tribal leaders to command manpower and the religious leaders to recruit, mobilise and legitimatize the uprising. The most prominent example is the Ghilzai rebellion 1881-82, 1886-88 where Mulla
Mushk-i-Alam[32] in 1882 propagated rebellion among the
Sulaiman Khel in Zurmat and Katawaz. After his death, his
son, Mulla Abdul Karim Andar, took over a leading role in
the uprising (against the imposition of land revenue in
1886) together with Muhammad Shah Hotaki (Kakar 1979), an
elder in the Hotaki section of Ghilzai.[33] These uprisings
were, in spite of the religious cloak they wore, rooted in
the defence of secular, material interests. This is clear
from the cases brought against the Amir from both the
tribes and the religious establishment, which mainly center-
ed around the imposition of taxes and the curtailment of
traditional privileges (see Kakar 1971). The religious
leaders' claim against the Amir was that he was too friend-
ly with the British, and his treatment of his own subjects
was too harsh. On this basis, the very respected Mulla
Najm al-Din, also known as the Hadda Mulla, denounced the
Amir as an infidel.[34]

However, although the *mullas* formed a distinct social
group, they in no way constituted a homogeneous group.
Their educational background differed widely and so did
their economic situation and their relationship to the local
population, with whom they were more closely associated than

with other *mullas*. The clergy's response to Amir Abdur
Rahman was not unanimous either. It could be as divergent
as in 1880, where Mulla Najm al-Din encouraged resistance
against the Amir among the Safis of Kunar, while Mulla
Khalil Mohmand[35] urged submission to the Amir. Equally so,
the Amir did have religious leaders to help him formulate
and carry out the policy, which the majority of the religious establishment opposed, including most venerated and
learned *mullas* like Mulla Mushk-i-Alam, the Hadda Mulla,
and others. Since the opposition to the Amir was not based
upon strictly religious matters, the response of the respec-
tive *mullas* was in most cases dependent upon the treatment
of and reaction among the population from which their followers came. An example of the union of tribal and cleri-
cal interests in a very secular deal is the agreement which
Amir Abdur Rahman in 1880 reached with Ghilzai elders concerning the withdrawal of British troops via Kandahar. It
is likely that the Amir obtained their consent with the
promise of high positions, for he subsequently conferred
the title of *khan-i-ulum* (the chief justice) upon Mulla
Abdul Karim, son of Mulla Mushk-i-Alam, and let the Ghilzai elder, Ismat Allah, act as a kind of Prime Minister for
a brief period (Kakar 1971, p. 66). Later on, of course,
the relationship with the Ghilzai worsened, a situation in
which Mulla Abdul Karim also played a prominent role.

In spite of Amir Abdur Rahman's ongoing controversy
with the clergy and his almost legendary mistrust and low
opinion of the *mullas*, there are many signs that the Amir
was personally a very religious man.[36] The remarkable
feature of Abdur Rahman was his profession of militant or-
thodoxy while at the same time securing the supremacy of
the state over the church. His political aim was to strength-
en religion, to impose the *sharia* and *sunna* all over the
country and to unify the country under one belief, the Hanafi Sunni doctrine[37] in the form which he found most con-
venient to the interests of the state. But full integration
of Islam into the state also required that the influence of

the *ulama* be curbed and that the clergy become servants of
the state through reforms in the legal, educational and
economic spheres.

Legal Reforms

Amir Abdur Rahman carried out important reforms in the legal field which contributed significantly to the strengthening of the state's (the Amir's)[38] control over society
in general and the religious establishment in particular.

Traditionally, the *qazis*, the judges, functioned only
in the cities, while in the countryside, where the government had little or no power, justice was administered by
anyone who was known to be well versed in Islamic law.
Disputes were referred to local *mullas*, who were paid small
fees for their settlement of cases, and even in the cities
few *qazis* had salaries from the treasury. In addition,
most cases of acknowledged crime were settled by *jirgas* and
the like without the intervention of *qazi* or other legal
institution. Taken as a whole, disputes were settled mainly in accordance with customary law (*rawaj*) rather than by
Islamic law (Kakar 1979, p. 50).

Amir Abdur Rahman attempted to enforce a unified legal system upon the country as a whole, in which all laws
should be in line with the *sharia*, whose interpretation
was the monopoly of the *qazi*. In addition, it was decreed
that nobody but the government-appointed (and salaried)
qazis and *muftis* was to settle legal cases. It is apparent
that customary law had no validity in the courts and that
the *qazis* were in a position to reject any ruling, even the
Amir's,which was not in line with Islamic law. While the
power of the *qazis* was thereby greatly increased[39], they
were not allowed to exercise their own judgement, and their
judgements had to be in accordance with classic authorities
on Islam. If a governor or a *qazi* were presented with a
case not specified in the codes, they were strictly ordered
not to exercise their own judgement but to refer the case
to the Amir for instruction (Ghani 1977, p. 61). However,

customary law and *jirgas* no doubt still operated (although
it is unknown to what extent) in the settlement of cases
outside the court (Kakar 1979, p. 52).

Although the decisions of the courts were based on
Islamic law, and the *khan-i-ulum* (Chief Justice) thus had
considerable power, the Amir seems to have bypassed his own
legal system when he felt it suited his or the state's interests. Having failed to influence the judgements of the
khan-i-ulum, the Amir chose to settle criminal cases himself while only legal and civil cases were referred to the
sharia courts. This division curtailed the actual jurisdiction of the *khan-i-ulum* considerably and the law lost
much of its significance (Kakar 1979, pp. 35-36). By re-
serving the right to appoint judges, by ensuring the participation of secular authorities (the district governors
in the district courts) in the judicial process, and by
preserving jurisdiction over cases punishable by death, the
Amir thus asserted the monarchy's supremacy and preeminent
rights in the dispensation of justice.

In fact, the Amir resumed the dual role of leader and
interpreter of Islam, in which capacity he struck at the
roots of the *ulama*'s power. As a ruler he argued that he,
for the sake of the nation and the faith, had the right to
define how Islamic laws were to be applied, and he exercised this right principally in the criminal and political
sphere, defining what was to be considered an offence and
what an appropriate punishment. The background for this
was the Islamic concept of *tazir* (deterrence) whose purpose was to deter others from similar conduct; however,
he frequently exceeded the proscribed (*Hanafi*) limits of
punishment by applying the death sentence[40] (Kakar 1979,
p. 167).

Another blow to the authority of the *ulama* was to remove from them the authority to call for *jihad*. *Jihad* or
ghaza could not be fought except under the orders and in-
structions of the ruler in Islam:

> "True Muslims must understand that Ghaza means
> to fight a defensive war in the case of any
> nation trying to take their country or stop their
> religion, and no Ghaza (religious war) can be
> fought except under the orders and instructions
> of the ruler of the country."
>
> (Mahomed 1900, II, p. 51)

And when the sovereign declared *jihad*, it was incumbent
(*farz-i-ayn*) on all able-bodied Muslims to defend the frontiers and the land of Islam themselves or to support the *ghazis*
with property (Kakar 1979, p. 177).

Educational Reforms

Mosques were the traditional centres of education, as in all
Muslim countries, where the *mulla* taught children the basic
tenets of Islam and the *ulama* instructed higher level students in *madrassas* attached to the principal mosques. The
Amir did not do much to raise the standard of religious
education, or education in general for that matter, and
although he did underline the need for secular education
for the survival of the Muslim states, his efforts were
mainly aimed at controlling education. He opened a royal
madrassa in Kabul where two hundred students were primarily
to be taught Islamic law, the expenses of lodging and education all to be met by the state. The study of *jihad* was
made a major subject on the curriculum in view of the importance that the Amir attached to this concept. The aim
was that these graduates from the royal *madrassa* should be
appointed the *qazis* and *muftis* of the future (Kakar 1979,
pp. 161-163). This policy would guarantee some uniformity
in education with the past, when the *ulama* were trained not
only in Afghanistan but to a large extent also in India,
Bukhara and Tashkent. However, the policy of uniformity
and control went further than that. A special committee,
directly appointed by the Amir, was entrusted with drafting
the general handbooks of religion as well as producing
pamphlets on various aspects of the faith. The Amir himself carefully scrutinised the content of each handbook or

pamphlet and sometimes even chose the appropriate verses
from the Quran. Only then did he issue orders for publication. In fact, some of the most important of these works
were written by the Amir himself.[41] By these means the
state controlled not only the educational institutions but
even the curriculum of those who would occupy some of the
most important positions in the country. The extent to
which this policy succeeded is illustrated by the fact that
one of the most important handbooks of this period, *Taqwim
Din* (The essence of Religion), is still in use today (Ghani
1977, pp. 72-74).

At a more popular level, state propagation of religious doctrines appeared. Roving *mullas* were appointed to
teach the population the fundamentals of Islam, and by the
authorisation of the *muhtasibs* they had the right to prose-
cute those who failed to observe the basic commandments
(Kakar 1979, pp. 161-163). Because of the Amir's attempts
to centralise and standardise the religious beliefs, the
position of the *muhtasib* gained considerable importance.
They not only looked after the religious and moral behaviour of the people, but also ensured that the local *imams*
performed their religious duties properly; and in case of
violation of regulations, they had the authority to imprison
or whip people:

> "...if people will not listen to their (the Muhtasibs)
> advice, they administer a certain number of lashes,
> because a nation which is not religious becomes
> demoralised and falls into ruin and decay, and
> misbehaviour makes people unhappy in this world
> and the next."
>
> (Mahomed 1900, II, p. 103)

The main religious practices being suppressed, apart from
shia doctrine, were the Sufi Orders and the so-called Indian
Wahabis. The Amir opposed the unorthodox practices of the
Sufi Orders on religious grounds and cut the state allowances to *khanaqahs*.[42] He was probably also influenced by
the fact that Sardar Muhammad Ishaq in Turkestan had received considerable support from the followers of the

Sufi Orders. As far as the Indian *Wahabis*[43] were concerned, there had for a hundred years (since Timur Shah) been a
special office at the court responsible for combating this
doctrine (Ghani 1978, pp. 282-83). This policy was rein-
forced by the Amir in his refusal to allow foreign *mullas*
to enter the country, and Afghans with foreign religious
education were generally mistrusted (Kakar 1979, Ghani
1978)[44]

The above is not intended to suggest that Amir Abdur
Rahman promoted any 'peculiar' Islam doctrines. On the contrary, his committee set up for examining the *mullas'* qualifications, under the chairmanship of Mulla Khosa of Laghman,
promoted only orthodox *sunni* Islam (*Hanafi*), based on the
authority of the *Quran*, the *Hadith* and the traditions of
famous scholars. However, the Amir took his advice primarily from the least known and most conservative *ulama* such as
Mulla Khosa because he had initially rejected the advice of
prominent people like Mulla Najm al-Din and Mulla Mushk-i-
Alam to show leniency towards his subjects (Kakar 1979, p.
44). The choice of relevant topics (for example, the Amir's
special adherence to the concept of *jihad*) was in harmony
with the centralising policy of the Amir and served to legitimise it (Ghani 1978, p. 272). The 'peculiar' element
in the religious policy was the way in which the standardisation and forced commitment to the official religious policy was carried out. The method applied to achieve these
objectives was a combination of the stick and the carrot,
the latter mainly consisting of economic benefits such as
state allowances and stipends to the *mullas*.

Economic Reforms

For Amir Abdur Rahman to be able to enforce his programmes
of religious-ideological standardisation upon the religious
establishment, he first had to break their economic independence. In 1885, he declared that most of those in receipt of grants for their alleged descent from the Prophet
or for their reputation for learning, had no real religious

knowledge. Therefore an examination of each one's creden-
tials was necessary to determine who actually deserved
such grants. In addition, all *auqaf* (religious endowments)
were to be nationalised by the state and their proceeds al-
lotted to the upkeep of the mosques.

In cases involving grants of land, beneficiaries were
forbidden to sell such land and the state asserted its claim
to re-occupy it whenever it saw fit to do so. An example
of this was the allowances granted to the descendants of
Sufi Islam Mirza Muhammad Omar (Seraj-ul-Tawarikh, Vol.III,
p. 1207). Furthermore, the traditional exemption of dignitaries from taxation on private landholdings was cancelled
and their land made subject to assessment.

This cutting of the economic resources of the clergy
was not principally aimed at increasing state revenue, but
rather at creating an economic dependency upon the state,
which could be used to exert political-ideological pressure on even the most prominent *mullas*. The return of privileges was made dependent on complete adherence to official religious policy, on non-participation in mystic orders
and on non-recruitment of followers (Ghani 1978, pp. 272-74).

These measures against the clergy should not probably
be viewed as predetermined steps in a grandiose plan, but
as results of a developing political situation. And the
execution of the policies was not without serious difficulties for the Amir. The clergy's initial opposition to
the Amir, based on their preference for Sardar Ayub, their
mistrust of Abdur Rahman's recognition by the British and
opposition to his very crude methods, led the Amir to use
economic measures to weaken their authority (Kakar 1979,
p. 153). He then began to reduce or completely stop the
allowances (*wazifas*) to certain *mullas*, while imprisoning
or killing others, but granting allowances to those who
would serve the state. The next step was the introduction
of the examining commissions under Mulla Khosa, the activities of which were further stressed after Mulla Abdul
Karim Andar's involvement in the Ghilzai rebellion in 1886.

The examination commissions were sent to several provinces, and *mullas* were summoned to Kabul from time to time. In Qandahar most of the *mullas* did not appear before the commission to be tested, and consequently their allowances were drastically reduced. Similarly, most Herat *mullas* did not respond to the summons and lost their allowances for a while.[45] Still failing to subdue the existing clergy in the provinces, the Amir sent deputations of his partisan *mullas* around the countryside to preach the accepted doctrines. Apart from the effects upon the population of this propagation, the measure also served to separate the *mullas* from their own communities (Kakar 1979, p. 153).

However, the fundamental problem of the Amir was that his general policy of centralisation of the country could not be carried out without the active support of the religious establishment. Since Islam was the only unifying factor in the nation, the only shared ideological 'raw material', the *ulama*, as the controllers of religious interpretations, had to endorse the policies of the Amir and the legitimacy of his rule, particularly since he had an ongoing conflict with the other power group - the tribal leaders with whom the clergy normally sided. At the end of the 1880's, by which time the most influential *mullas* had either been liquidated or forced out of the country, the Amir considered it inadvisable to alienate the remainder (Kakar 1979, p. 155). Instead he took more active steps to ensure their dependency upon the state and to make them serve it in return for receiving allowances.

After almost a decade of confrontations and suppressions, many of the *mullas* now accepted the Amir's authority. The Amir's need of the *mullas* and their mutual understanding was also furthered by the Hazara War in which the Amir had no problem in obtaining the clergy's support for *jihad*, and the conquest of Kafiristan, after which many *mullas* were employed in conversion activities. All these internal developments, as well as the Russian seizure of Panjdeh (1885) and later overtures about Wakhan, caused the clergy

to rally round the Amir for the defence of Islam and the
nation against the infidels. And ultimately the Amir managed to obtain a *fatva* to the effect that whoever made ex-
cuses to avoid serving the king of Islam (i.e. the Amir)
was, according to Muslim law, an infidel (Kakar 1979, pp.
155-56).

The effect of the Amir's legal, educational and economic reforms is not easily evaluated, as it is impossible
to find out to what extent his *fermans* and so on were actually enforced. He did however manage to cut some of the independent economic resources of the clergy (such as *sadaqa*,
zakat)[46] subject it to taxation and hence create greater
dependency upon the allowances (*wazifa*) from the State. In
general, the harsh taxation policy and even harsher repression of political opponents[47] resulted in the authority of
the state being imposed upon the country to a hitherto unprecedented degree while the power of the three traditional
power groups, the *sardars*, the tribal leaders and the religious leaders was curtailed. In the view of the Amir, the
means used were legitimised by the goal, which was the creation of unity in the nation, an essential value. ("Do not
ye know what blessings the true faith of Islam has awarded
to you; uniting your scattered tribes and communities into
one brotherhood?"[48]

Ideology of the State

> "As God wished to relieve Afghanistan from
> foreign aggression and internal disturbances,
> He honoured this, His humble servant, by placing
> him in this responsible position and He caused
> him to become absorbed in thoughts of the wel-
> fare of the nation and inspired him to be devoted
> to the progress of this people...for the welfare
> and true faith of the Holy Prophet Mahomed."
>
> (Mahomed 1900, II, p. 80)

It is apparent that Amir Abdur Rahman from the beginning
ascribed divine sanction as well as divine purpose to his
rule. As previously noted, he was not the first Afghan
ruler to do so, but he seems to have gone a step further by

claiming the divine right of kingship. From many sayings of the Prophet and Quranic quotations, an elaborate doctrine was constructed, the essence of which was that the kings of religion were the vicars of the Prophet, the shadow of God and the shield against unbelief (*kufr*) and rebellion (Kakar 1979, p. 8; Gregorian 196, p. 130; Mohammad 1900, II, p. 2, 15, 50, 198, 200). It was stated that Allah had ordained that the safeguard of religion and of the honour of the people of Islam depended on the organisation of the kingdom (Risala-i-Muwa-issa, quoted from Kakar 1979, p. 8). This was the most successful attempt of any Afghan ruler, before or after, to claim the religious legitimation of his rule. While the Amir in all his policies aimed at surpassing the tribal-state model as a source of legitimacy of his rule as well as in his actual politics in an attempt to make the state independent of the tribe, he did not directly deny the people's right to choose their ruler (the *jirga* principle): the people have full authority to choose the king, and kings who have been forced upon the people against their wish have lost not only the kingdom but their heads as well (Mahomed 1900, II, p. 2). But he insisted that only divine guidance could lead them to choose a true and legitimate ruler.[49] The strength, the authority, and the legitimacy of the monarch emanated from God alone. Hence the tribal-state model of legitimacy was not in opposition to the Islamic model, but was, in the Amir's formulations, subordinate to it.

Here also is the explanation of why the Amir, in spite of all the confrontations with the *ulama*, still needed them so badly. He could only establish the religious legitimisation of his rule, and impose the Islamic ideological concepts upon the tribes, if he had the cooperation of the *ulama*. Hence, while the Amir was striking at the root of the *ulama* power to consolidate the absolute monarchy, the sanction of the *ulama* was needed to legitimise the rule over the population. A case in point is the Amir's relationship to the prominent (Hadda) Mulla Najm al-Din.

The Hadda Mulla was one of the most influential religious dignitaries of the time, reputed to have had more than a hundred thousand followers. His followers were particularly in East Afghanistan and among the *mullas*, his influence being due to his learning and piety. At first the Amir, mistrusting him for his great influence, tried to obtain a *fatva* declaring the Hadda Mulla was a *Wahabi*. Failing in this, the Amir tried to win him over, asking him to try to persuade the Ghilzais to desist from fighting. But the Hadda Mulla wanted to get guarantees that the Amir would show leniency towards the tribesmen. The Amir rejected this proposal and arranged to have the Mulla killed. However, the Mulla discovered the plot and managed to escape and settled in eastern Afghanistan beyond the reach of the Amir. From here he continued to denounce the Amir for his cruelty and damage to Islam because of his contact with the British and other Europeans. In spite of this, the Amir did not give up the idea of winning over such an important religious leader and he continued to try to persuade the Hadda Mulla to come to Kabul "to promulgate the Mohammadan Law afresh." In a letter of invitation to him, the 'Amir stated: "I consider the presence in my Durbar of men like you, who are perfect in devotion and religion, as a means of success and guidance for eternity." However, the Mulla wisely resisted the offer and kept out of reach (Kakar 1979, p. 156). Ultimately, by 1890, the Hadda Mulla and the Amir were working for the same objective. As a prelude to the conquest of Kafiristan, the Amir (in about 1886) lent his official blessing to the *jihad* movement of Mulla Khalil and the Khan of Asmar, and by 1890 the Hadda Mulla allowed his followers to join the conversion activities (Kakar 1971, p. 188). However, no rapprochement seems to have come about between the Amir and the Mulla.

It was no accident that the Hadda Mulla and Amir Abdur Rahman could find a common ground in the *jihad* in Kafiristan. The tradition of *jihad* in Afghanistan was always strong, and the rulers of Afghanistan frequently invoked the principles of *jihad* against their non-Muslim adversaries. Abdur Rahman extended *jihad* more than any other ruler had done, as a means of mobilising the army and the people against the possible foreign invasion of Afghanistan and the ruin of Islam by the Christian powers - and as a means of creating a sense of unity within the nation. In the movement of *jihad* initiated by the Amir, the stress was placed on safeguarding 'the land of Islam' and the 'frontiers of Islam' from the infidels. Following the conquest of Kafiristan in 1896, the elders and the *ulama* conferred on him the title of *ghazi* and of *Zia al-Millat w'al-Din* (the light of the nation and religion). Apart from the Kafiristan conquest, the classic notion of *jihad* was giving way to a *jihad* movement of a much more defensive character.[50] This also had other consequences: the necessity for organising the state and the obedience of the Muslims to their kings was stressed. Only when the kingdom of the people of Islam was organised did war and peace with the infidels become possible, for a kingdom without a king was said to be open to invasion and destruction (Kakar 1979, p. 178).

Hence, for the defence of the nation (*millat*) and the faith (*din*) the Afghans should pay obedience to the Amir. God would bless those respecting the ruler, and cause misery to those harbouring open or secret contempt for him. The subjects must help their king to strengthen the Islamic community, and must oppose all those fomenting dissention or rising in rebellion against the authority of the monarch (Taqwim Din, quoted in Ghani 1977, p. 81).

The attempts of the Amir to harness the Islamic doctrines and ideals to support the state and legitimise his own rule was applied to a variety of concepts which he, in the position of 'Interpreter of Islam' dealt with in various religious treatises which he either wrote himself or had published. However, those state-controlled religious doctrines did not only set out the general duties of the believers, but were in many cases very specific and closely related to the actual situation in Afghanistan. The most

significant Islamic virtues were said to be: giving *zakat*,
taking part in *jihad* service at the borders of the Islamic
State and obedience to the ruler (Ghani 1977, p. 76).

The religious obligation which was most emphatically
put forth was that of *jihad*. It is the absolute duty of
every Muslim to volunteer for *jihad*, and denial of the
principle was to be interpreted as a sure sign of infideli-
ty (Taqwim Din, p. 7, quoted in Ghani 1977, p. 77). To
fulfil this obligation, the Muslim must join the army of
Islam, one day of service being equal to sixty years of
prayers. The Prophet's command makes it obligatory for one
of every two men of a tribe to join the army, but, it was
pointed out, because of the leniency of the Afghan Amir,
only one out of every twenty men had to report for service
(Targhib al-Jihad: pp. 30-31 , quoted in Ghani 1977, p. 78).
In this way, the principle of *jihad* became directly linked
with the system of regular, general conscription to the
army, which no ruler before Abdur Rahman had been able to
enforce upon the tribesmen.[51] To strengthen the morale of
the soldiers and the spirit of *jihad* among them, each regi-
ment had a *mulla* who recited passages from the *Najiyya* and
the *Hidayat al-Shajan*, booklets especially prepared for this
purpose (Kakar 1979, p. 99).

The concept of *zakat* (legally obligatory alms - 1/40th
to be paid by believers to the poor and needy) was used to
justify the imposition of taxes, and the collection of *zakat*
was one of the ruler's duties (Taqwim Din, quoted in Ghani
1977, p. 81). The *mullas* used to receive *zakat* as well as
sadaqa (religious charity) which the Amir now wanted transferred to the state. Some *sayyids* from Herat wrote a peti-
tion to the Amir asking to be exempted from paying taxes as
they once were. The Amir turned down the request with the
following verse from the Quran: "Do your prayers and pay
your *zakat*", which prevented the Amir from exempting the
mullas; he also referred to the need for money for the
army which should defend the country against the Kafirs
(Seraj ul-Tawarikh III, p. 787). At times the Amir had to

enter into more secular bargaining to obtain money. After
years of conflict with the clergy, in which their state
allowances (*wazifas*) were cut or reduced, the Amir resumed
the *wazifas* on the condition that the *mullas* serve the state
and hand over to the state whatever they received in *zakat*
and *sadaqa* from the people (Kakar 1979, pp. 84 and 155).

As collector of revenue, the Amir considered himself
to be the '*naib* of the Prophet' (vicar or viceroy of the
Prophet) since the revenue was a part of the '*bayt al-mal*'
(public property) and was to be spent on the protection of
frontiers of the country and the honour of the religion and
faith. Consequently, any negligence in the payment of revenue was tantamount to disobedience to the commands of God
and it was his duty as the ruler of Islam to ensure that
this did not happen. Similarly, the Amir explained the increases in land revenue as the commands of God. However,
the religious justification for taxation did not alter the
fact that, during the reign of Amir Abdur Rahman, the burden of taxation grew so heavy on the population that
thousands of families (in East Afghanistan supposedly up
to ten per cent) all over the country left their land and
roamed around as beggers and the like (Kakar 1979, Chapter
4).

It was mentioned earlier that the conflicts between the
Amir and the religious establishment was mainly rooted in
secular and material interests rather than in disagreements
concerning religion as such. In fact, by imposing Islam as
the ultimate authority in all matters, promoting orthodox
Sunni Islam and stressing the concept of *jihad* so strongly,
the Amir was actually promoting the interests of the *ulama*
of the country, since the influence and authority of *qazis*,
muftis and others was increased. The cause of conflict was
not in fact the ideological content of the Amir's policy,
but his attempts to transfer the alliance and dependency of
the religious dignitaries from the tribes to the state. On
the one hand this would curtail the independence of the
clergy, but on the other hand it would increase their

authority and sphere of influence in the population. Earlier the *mullas* had to accept the coexistence and often pre-
dominance of *pashtunwali* and *rawaj* over Islam, while the policy of the Amir clearly stressed the ultimate authority of
Islam. The Islamisation of Amir Abdur Rahman, his justification of revenue and tax collection by the demands of Islam,
has a certain resemblance to present-day attempts to impose
sharia on modern society, such as the attempts to 'rehabili-
tate' the *zakat* system in Pakistan under the spiritual guidance of Maulana Abdul Ala Maududi.[52)]

In fact, the Amir was more orthodox and radical in his
policy than the majority of *ulama* would have dared to be,
and rejected the advice of leading *ulama* to show leniency.
The background of this more mild and flexible attitude on
the part of the traditional *ulama* should no doubt be found
in their close association with the people, i.e. their alliances with and dependency upon, for example, the tribal population.

However, it should be stressed that it was not Islam
as such which was promoted during the Amir's reign, but exclusively the *Hanafi Sunni* sect, which he tried to turn into
a state religion. The Islamisation process had to take such
a narrow and specific form because it was carried out by a
secular ruler for whom state control and centralisation was
of greater consequence than religious-philosophical disputes. The extreme narrowness of the official definition
of Islam is illustrated by the fact that the Amir declared
jihad against the *shii* minority, the Hazaras and Qizilbash,
and recruited volunteers by promising loot and slaves. This
was a most serious religious crime, since *jihad* can only be
declared against non-believers, and Muslims can never be
taken as slaves according to islam. The fact that the Amir
got the willing support of the *ulama* in these deeds must be
a subject for continued embarrassment for later Afghan *ulama*.
A consequence is that this unholy policy has embittered the
life of the *shii* minority in Afghanistan ever since.

Evaluating the Amir's reasons for this policy, it seems

clear that he was in no way guided by any religious fanaticism (although he exploited the fanaticism of others) in his persecution of the *shiis*. He, in fact, was ready to have anybody pronounced as infidel provided it served his purpose; he even attempted to have a *jihad* declared against the Sunni Ghilzai, and the orthodox Wahibis alongside his suppression of the unorthodox Sufi Orders. No matter how honest the Amir's personal beliefs may have been, in his national policy Islam served as a means to achieving the cherished aim of the absolute and centralised monarchy rather than being an end in itself.

Summary

The reign of Amir Abdur Rahman must be evaluated against the background of his determination to break the structural limitations of the tribal state and create a modern state apparatus in Afghanistan, a purpose in which to a large extent he succeeded. This policy was to break the independence of the traditional power groups in society, the royal lineage, the tribal leaders and the religious establishment, and to turn them into groups whose basic interests, economically and politically, were merged with those of the state. As shown, this was done through subduing these groups with (or with the threat of) force and by curtailing their economic basis, and consequently securing their allegiance to the state through allowances and favours, so that their position of power and authority was derived from and dependent upon the state. Because of this the socio-economic structure of Afghan society as a whole did not change during the reign of Amir Abdur Rahman; his policy was aimed only at the restructuring of power relations between the ruling groups of society and the state. However, for such an enterprise to succeed and to be not entirely dependent upon the use of physical force (i.e. the army), the justification of legitimacy of power vis-à-vis the total population was essential. Hitherto the tribal state model had been the dominant one in society, and the Amir's

political and economic policy was to replace that model by
an Islamic model of legitimacy of power. To base the legitimacy of this rudimentary modern-type state upon Islam was
the most obvious, if not the only choice open to the Amir.
Islam was the only common denominator in a very heterogeneous society, forming as it did the primary cultural heritage
among all groups of society, with a strong popular tradition
whose ultimate authority could not be challenged. An added
benefit in the present situation was that the Islamic tradition also contained the possibility of sanctioning an absolute monarchy.

Since the religious establishment as a group claimed a
monopoly on the interpretation of Islam, it was obvious
that the Amir's policy could not succeed without subjecting
this group to state control. It was also inevitable that
Islam as such should gain an even stronger position in society than it had hitherto enjoyed, since it was being util-
ised as the state-supporting ideology. In establishing the
hegemony of the state-sanctioned interpretations of Islam,
the whole educational system was organised for this purpose,
and so were the legal, executive and legislative powers.
The religious beliefs and practices were controlled and
standardised to comply with the State Church of Hanafi Sunni
Islam.

The religious content or elements in the ideological
discourse sanctioning the centralising policy of the Amir
was the ultimate authority of the Quran, the *Hadith* , the
tradition of famous Muslim scholars and Orthodox *sunni*
jurisprudence in general. However, the discourse into which
these concepts were integrated was determined by the secular, political goals of the central state, and not by any
religious goals. In fact, in the following decades Afghan
intellectuals such as Mahmud Tarzi took a stand upon the
very same sources as the Amir, but as they favoured a more
liberal internal policy they emphasised the egalitarian and
liberal spirit of early Islam rather than the jurisprudence
(Ghani 1977, p. 74). The comparative success of the Amir's

political use of Islam was due to several factors. In the
internal Afghan situation the precondition for establishing
ideological hegemony was the interpellation of concepts
from the strongest cultural heritage. And, by applying orthodox *sunni* doctrine in their religious policy no challenge of religious interpretations by the clergy was possible. In external policy Afghanistan's location as a
buffer state between the two Christian powers strongly
favoured the Amir's extensive use of the concept of *jihad*
and all other concepts which could be related to the defence of the faith.

Islam, as propagated by the Afghan state during the
reign of Amir Abdur Rahman served a specific political purpose. But the impact was wider since it strengthened an
already existing self-contained and conservative popular
attitude towards the outside world.

Notes:

1) "The Russians continued to conquer and occupy the Asian khanates, or reduced them to political or economic vassalage through treaties and the control of trade. The British, busily consolidating their gains in India, looked nervously again towards Afghanistan. In 1869, the Khan of Bokhara became a Tsarist vassal. Therefore, only one year after Sher Ali returned to power in Kabul, Russian influence reached the banks of the Amu Darya. A Paper written by Sir Henry Rawlinson in July 1868, and at first rejected, would, ten years later, become the cornerstone for the British "Forward Policy" in Asia. The main points of the paper were: occupy Quetta; gain control of the Afghan area by subsidizing the Amir in Kabul; establish a permanent British Mission in Kabul to keep the Russians out" (Ghose 1960, p. 10, from Dupree 1973, p. 404).

2) "The two Afghan wars seriously damaged the country's meagre economy, especially the urban economy. The population and the economy of Kabul and of the Kandahar region declined sharply; the province of Herat also suffered enormous material losses. The modest achievements of the Amirs Dost Mohammad and Sher Ali were undone" (Gregorian 1969, p. 126).

3) For a discussion of *pashtunwali* and its relationship to the wider social environment see, for example, Barth 1969.

4) Leon Poullada (1973, p. 19) describes what he calls "the politics of tribal power" and discusses what he considers the five basic conflict types in society.

4a) The development of the model of the legitimation of transmission of power in traditional Muslim society has been carried out by Dr. Mehdi Mozaffari. The adaption of the model to Afghanistan is my own responsibility.

5) Dost Muhammad resumed this title when he, in 1834, declared *jihad* against the Sikh ruler Ranjit Singh who had taken Peshawar. Thousands of people volunteered for the *jihad* (Kaye 1851, Vol I, p. 129). In 1839, Dost Muhammad's attempts to gain support against Shah Shuja were based upon an appeal to religion (Shah Shuja being a puppet of the British) and upon an appeal to tribal loyalties. Although he almost forced the *ulama* of Qandahar to issue a *fatva* in his support, it had but little effect, since the majority Sunni population was against' Dost Muhammad's Qizilbash (*shia*) connection and the *ualama* in general was discontented because of his reduction or abolition of their allowances (Yapp 1962, p. 521).

6) "Justice is administered in cities by the Cauzy, the Mooftees, the Ameeni Mehkemeh, and the Darogha of the Adawlut.
   In civil suits the Cauzy receives complaints, and sends a summons by an officer of his own to the defendant. The cause is tried according to the rules and forms prescribed by the Shirra, or Mohommedan law, modified by certain acknowledged parts of the Pooshtoonwullee, or customary law...
   The Ameeni Mehkemeh receives charge of deposits.
   The Darogha in Adawlut is supervisor over the whole, and his duty is to see that all proceedings are conformable to law.
   In criminal complaints.... The criminal is generally first brought to the Sirdar, and the Cauzy's sentence in all important cases is executed by him: this gives the Sirdar a degree of power which is particularly felt when he disagrees with the Cauzy...
   The Cauzees are appointed by the King, at the recommendation of the Imaum of the household.
   A few only have salaries from the treasury. There is,however, in some places, if not in all, a small tax imposed on every family in the district, which goes entirely to the Cauzy...
   The Mooftis have a fee on every opinion they give,..." (Elphinstone 1839, II, pp.262-64).

7) "The Mohtesib inflicts the punishment prescribed by the Mussulmaun law on persons who drink wine, or are guilty of similar irregularities: ...The Mohtesib is always a Moollah". (Elphinstone, 1839, II, pp. 264-65).

8) Ghani (1977, p. 42) writes that by 1879 most of the inhabitants paid revenue, although the system of taxation varied from region to region and between ethnic groups. An example is given which illustrates that a large share of this revenue-income is spent on the upkeep of the aristocracy and the religious establishment. The permanent local obligations on the government of Jalalabad is classified as follows:

   (a) *wazifas* - allowances in cash and grain made to men of priestly and religious classes. Every learned and religious person in the district appears to be in receipt of a *wazifa*.
   (b) *malikana* - small allowances in cash or kind granted to the headmen of villages.
   (c) *takhfif* - remission of revenue.
   (d) *jagirs* - assignments of revenue in favour of certain khans, sardars and maliks.
   (e) *tankhwal-i-wilayati* - includes all the allowances made to independent and semi-independent tribes - and the salaries granted to the officials and chief men of the district. (Ghani 1977, pp. 42-43).

9) Bellew (1864/1977, pp. 184-189) gives a list of people of religious knowledge or renown:

Mullahs:

imam - leader of congregation belonging to a mosque.
mullah - ordinary priest
shaikh - relinquishes worldly pleasures, becomes *murid* (disciple) of a saint.
talib - mixed class of itinerants.

All four groups supported by the produce of rent-free lands attached to mosques and by periodical presents of clothing and food.

Astanadars:

"Place possessors" - people whose ancestors acquired sainthood among the Afghans.
sayad - Arab descent, receives considerable land gifts.
pir - Pashtun descent, in charge of a shrine (*ziarat*) and has a share in the land belonging to it.
mian - "*hamsaya*" descent, privileges like pirs, but on a smaller scale.
sahibzada - like a *pir* and *mian*, but with an ancestor of less importance.
(See also Einzman 1977).

10) The Naqshbandiya, Qadiriya, Chistiya orders are represented in Afghanistan (Utas 1980 also refers to traces of the Suhravardiya order). Elphinstone (1839, I, pp. 272-73) mentions that sufism was growing strong in Kabul, and that it was not disregarded by the government but was despised by the *mullas*. Turkestan also appears to have had strong adherence to sufism (Kakar 1979). (For a description of the Afghan Sufi Orders, see Utas 1980).

11) Canfield (1973, pp. 95-107) gives a brief summary of the pressures exerted on the Hazara-areas by the Kabul-rulers and Pashtun groups during the last couple of centuries (see also Masson 1842, Burnes 1834, Elphinstone 1839, Vambery 1868 and Raverty 1888).

12) Dost Muhammad followed a divide-and-rule policy aimed chiefly at preventing an alliance between the politically and economically influential Qizilbash of Kabul and the Hazaras. He published the Qizilbash descent of his mother and intervened to settle Qizilbash conflicts with the *sunni* community in Kabul while he encouraged *sunni* animosity towards the Hazaras which was useful for his own military goals in Hazarajat (Gregorian 1969, p. 77).

13) "In the Imami theological set-up the Imam is God's
deputy on earth and a part of his divine being. From
this derives the dogmatic principle of the *isma*,
which means that those belonging to the family of the
Prophet are believed to be free from error and sin.
The divine inspiration passes on to the first born
child of each generation or to the eldest son whose
mother too is of holy descent. The Sayyed is - in
continuing line - mediator between mankind and the
Imam, or God" (Kopecky 1982, p. 90).

14) Ferrier 1857, pp. 220-221, mentions the conflicts
and divisions among the Hazaras.

15) *ghazi*: warrior against the infidels
shahid: martyr.

16) Peters (1979) discusses the concept of *jihad*, showing
how it has changed from the early days of Islam, when
any war against unbelievers was a *jihad* until today
when the widening gulf between politics and religion
has made the call for *jihad* dependent upon its political expediency rather than upon the objective conditions laid down by the *sharia*. The word"*jihad*",
however, in modern Arabic stands for a rather vague
concept which need not have anything to do with religion or warfare.

17) For example, India under British rule was (at times)
considered *dar al-harb* (territory of war) whereby
Muslims in India were obliged to rebel and entitled
to the support of the Muslim brethren within *dar
al-Islam*. In Afghanistan at the time of the Mutiny
in 1857, there was a popular movement for the support
of the Indian Muslims.

18) Such a reaction of total rejection of European culture
in all its aspects has found its expression in most
Muslim societies. Among the Muslims of British India,
for example, Sayid Ahmad Bareilly and his Indian
Wahabism exemplified such a turning away from the material world and towards the essentials of Islam.

19) *Fatva* is an evaluation of a religious question or a
binding religious pronouncement given by a *mufti*.

20) M. Parmelee, in H.P. Fairchild: Dictionary of Sociology, Philosophical Library, New York 1944, p. 144).

21) Laclau (1977) is basing his assertion on Althusser's notion of ideology. However, the ideological class struggle, as discussed by Althusser and Poulantzas, is related to capitalist societies, where the economic position of the ruling class is paralleled by its hegemonic position within the political and ideological state apparatuses. This model cannot be transferred to the societies of the Third World, where the development of the state has taken another course and where its form and function is radically different.

22) In determining the relation between ideologies and the class struggle Laclau (1977) restricts the term "class struggle" to antagonisms which are intelligible on the abstract level of the mode of production, while other antagonisms are only intelligible at the level of a concrete social formation. This means that not all confrontations of classes can be considered class struggles - for example, conflicts between the petty bourgeoisie and the feudal class.

23) A class ideology, functioning as such through constituting a system of specific interpellations, is not the fully-fledged ideology of that class; it is just one of its abstract and necessary conditions (Laclau 1977, pp. 110-111).

24) Amir Abdur Rahman, his reign and policies, has been dealt with in extenso by Kakar (1971, 1979), Ghani (1977, 1978). Gregorian (1969) deals with both internal and external aspects of Abdur Rahman's reign and so does Dupree (1973), while Adamec (1967) deals with the external aspects only. Apart from these, a host of contemporary writers have written about the Amir, among these numerous British political reporters. The autobiography of Amir Abdur Rahman, compiled by Mir Munshi Sultan Mohamed Khan (1900) is a very valuable and illuminating document; for an evaluation of its status as a contemporary source, see Kakar (1971). A most important local source is Faiz Mohammad: Seraj-ul-Tawarikh.

25) All Abdur Rahman's campaigns are dealt with by Kakar (1977).

26) "Because of their kinship and solidarity to the royal family, His Majesty has chosen the members of the Mohammadzai lineage to be superior to the Ghilzai and Durrani tribes and that they should be more prosperous. Therefore, it is decided that, in order that their life be more comfortable than that of other people, each man should receive a yearly salary of four hundred rupees and each woman three hundred, so that the foundation of the State and this dynasty be stable". (Seraj-ul-Tawarikh: 914, quoted from Ghani 1977, p. 122).

27) The Army alone, according to the Amir, absorbed about 78 per cent of the total income of the state (Kakar 1979, p. 230). Already Amir Sher Ali had reduced the sardars' power by creating a standing army of about 56 000, converted into regular troops and paid in cash. The army was mainly recruited among the Ghilzai and Pashto became the language of the army (Kakar 1971, p. 4) - and still is today.

28) "It is then apparent that customary laws had no validity in the courts and that the qazis were in a position to reject any ruling, even the amir's firmans, not in line with Islamic laws... To what extent the jirgas functioned and to what extent the Shari'a actually was enforced cannot be determined, although it is clear that during this period Shari'a was more extensively applied than at any other time in Afghanistan". (Kakar 1979, p. 52).

29) See Kakar (1979: Chapter IV) and for imposition of taxes, see Kakar (1971). Land revenue and a multitude of other taxes were increased to an unprecedented degree.

30) See for example Kakar (1971, p. 174) about the colonisation of Hazarajat, and Kakar (1979, pp. 131-135) for the colonisation of Northwestern Afghanistan.

31) See Kakar (1971: Chapters VI and VII). Concerning the Kafiristan campaign, Kakar (1971, p. 188) writes that Mullah Khalil, who was a very influential and politically active person, and the Khan of Asmar had an ongoing *jihad* against Kafiristan, which the Amir gave official blessing to. By 1890 also Mullah Najm al-Din, known as the Hadda Mullah, also gave support to the Campaign.

32) Mullah Mushk-i-Alam Akhundzada, whose real name was Din Mohammad, had declared *jihad* when the British in 1879 occupied Kabul. He was identified with the Andar section of the Ghilzai and had an enourmous influence with the *mullas* and people of Ghazni, Kabul, Laghman and particularly among the Mohmands and was respected throughout the country on account of his religious knowledge and the establishment of *madrassas*. The influence and respect was increased by the fact that he was a wealthy man, receiving allowances from the Amir in Kabul, presents from his followers and owning large tracts of revenue free land (Kakar 1971, p. 16). Mullah Mushk-i-Alam was a leading figure in the so-called National Party (see Kakar 1971) and his main aversion to Amir Abdur Rahman seems to have been the latters connection to or acceptance by the British. However, ultimately the Mullah reached an agreement with the British to support the Amir and cool down his *ghazis*, provided the British leave Afghanistan (Kakar 1971, pp. 49-50).

33)   In dealing with the Ghilzai rebellion in 1887, the
Amir tried to enlist the *mullas'* support. Five
hundred *mullas* from Logar, Laghman and neighbour-
hood of Kabul met to discuss the matter and Mulla
Khosa of Laghman drafted a *fetva* sanctioning *jihad*
against the Ghilzai. The great majority of *mullas,*
however, told the Amir that "he had killed all the
chiefs who could help him, that he could expect
nothing from them, except prayers, and that he was
justified in fighting those who were the most dangerous to Islam". (Kakar 1979, p. 155).

34)   This denounciation was in connection with the Shinwari
rebellion, where the Amir at a time tried to use the
Mulla as peace negotiator. The Hadda Mulla was also
politically active across the border in inciting to
rebellion in Swat, Bajaur and Dir - together with
the "Mad Mullah of Swat" (see Warburton 1900, pp.
290-299) and Hamilton (1906, pp. 415-417, 442, 479-
488).

35)   Warburton (1900, p. 218) describes Mulla Khalil as "a
regular firebrand of the Afghan war of 1878-80" pensi-
oned with 5000 rupees from the Afghan army. He was
stirring up the Mohmands to resist the British Kabul-
River Survey 1890-91.

36)   In the autobiography of Abdur Rahman (Mahomed 1900)
there are numerous evidence of the beliefs of the Amir.
While his claim that the Prophet and the Four Compa-
nions had appeared to him in a revelation, chosing
him as future Amir (Vol. II, p. 232) might be somewhat tainted by political aims, there is not the
same reason to doubt his sincerity when describing
how God helped him to learn to read and write over
night (Vol. I, pp. 37-39).

37)   This policy involved the campaigns of conversion of
the inhabitants of Kafiristan, and attempts to com-
pel the Qizilbash *imami-shias* to follow Sunna. However, the persecution of *shias* really took its start
with the Hazara war, when the Amir accused the Qizilbash as well as the *mujtahid* of Mashad as being in-
stigators of the war (Kakar 1979, pp. 158-159).

38)   The Amir did give some concessions to democratic
principles, as he formed a constitutional assembly
made up of representatives from three groups: *sardars,*
khwanin mulki (khans and landed proprietors) and *mullas.*
The selection of members were subject to the Amir's approval and the assembly had neither executive nor legislative power. The Amir also established a selected executive body (*khilwat*) as a kind of cabinet, but
it was equally powerless; it's only function was to
execute the will of the Amir (Gregorian 1969, p. 134).

39) For a specification of the authority of the *qazi*, see Ghani (1977, pp. 52-54).

40) Here the Amir actually followed the Maliki law school's principle of punishment requiring that the punishment should fit the nature of the crime and the character of the offender, including the death penalty in certain "suitable cases" (Kakar, 1979, p. 167).

41) Ghani (1977, pp. 140-141) provides a list over the writings of the Amir as well as books written under the supervision of the Amir. On religious matters the following can be mentioned:

Written by the Amir:

Aina-i-Jehan Numa (1899) (The World Revealing Mirror).
Mir'at ul-'Oqul (1893) (On Degrees of Wisdom).
Nasieh Namcha (1885) (Booklet of Advice).
Pand Nama Dunia wa Din (1885) (Book of Advice on Religion and Worldly Affairs).
Sar Reshta-i-Islamia Rum (1886) (The Organization of the Islamic Ottoman State).

Written under the supervision of the Amir:

Abdul Rauf: Kalimat Amir ul-Bilad Fi Targhib al-Jihad (1886) (Message of the Ruler of the Contry on the Encouragement of Holy War).
Abdur Rahman, Qazi: Resala Hujat Kawiya Dar Rad Abtal Akayed Wahabia (1871) (A Collection of Strong Arguments Rejecting the False Wahabi Doctrine).
Abdur Rahman, Qazi: Resala Nadjia (1889) (Book of Righteousness).
Abdul Qadir, Qazi: Tohaftu Ulama (1875) (Gift to the Learned).
Abu Bakr et al.: Taqwim Din (1888) (The Essence of Religion).
Azizi, Mir Saif-ud-Din: Nasaieh Subian (1885) (Advice to the Young).

42) An exception was the descendants of Sufi Islam of Karrukh of Herat, one of the most influential religious centres of that province (still in existence today). Sufi Islam had come from Bokhara and established a *khanaqah* of the Naqshbandi order. The Amir's respect for him, and hence for his descendants, was based on Sufi Islam having sacrificed his life in declaring *jihad* against the Persians for their attact on Herat (Kakar, 1979, p. 152).

43) Kakar (1979, p. 138 writes, that what Amir Abdur Rahman was generally referring to as Wahabis at this time in fact was not the real Wahabis (disciples of Mohammad b. Abd al-Wahab) but the followers of Sayyid Ahmad Bareilly (the Indian Wahabis) as well as the followers of Mirza Ghulam Ahmad of Qadian, i.e. the Ahmadiyyas. The latter was denounced as *kafirs* due to their rejection of the notion of the seal of prophecy.

44)   In a *firman* the Amir declared "that every mullah whose
      whereabouts, nationality and parentage are not known
      shall be expelled from the country, so that no stran-
      ger may come and foment disturbances" (Kakar 1979,
      p. 154). In Seraj-ul-Tawarikh (Vol. III, p. 797) the
      following incidence is reported: A certain Safdar Ali
      from Jeddah, staying in India, applied to the Amir
      for permission to enter Afghanistan for teaching pur-
      poses. The Amir replied that the Afghan government
      could not recognise him, since it could know neither
      his sect nor religion - whether he was a *kharaji* or
      a *shii*, a complete infidel or a true Muslim, or a
      Jew or a Christian or a Naturalist or a Philosopher,
      an imitator or a *mujtahid*. After this message, nothing
      more was heard of Safdar Ali, who had understood "that
      the Afghans with such a pious king shall never leave
      the road of *Haq* to embrace another religion". A simi-
      lar incidence is reported where a Sayyid Muhammad
      Rashid Baghdadi, a reciter (*qari*) of Quran, asks for
      permission to come to Kabul; the refusal to him was
      also in no uncertain terms (ibid., p. 956).

45)   Ultimately, even the most prominent religious digni-
      taries form Herat did submit to be checked by the
      Examination Commission. In Seraj-ul-Tawarikh (III,
      p. 516) is reported that Mian Muhammad Khan Sahibzada,
      Mir Murtaza Khan of Gazargah and Mirza Muhammad Omar
      Khan (son of the Hazarat Sahib of Karrukh) were going
      to Kabul to be examined by a commission consisting of
      Mulla Sayyid Muhammad Khan, Mulla Dad Muhammad Khan,
      Mulla Abdullah and Mulla Qutbuddin Khan who were as-
      signed by the Amir. The aim was to check the quali-
      fications (i.e. knowledge of *fiq* (jurisprudence)) of
      these very prominent religious leaders so their al-
      lowances (*wazifas*) could be determined in proportion
      to their qualifications.

46)   *sadaqa*: religious charity
      zakat: obligatory alms - 1/40 to be paid by the belie-
      vers to the poor and needy.

47)   Amir Abdur Rahman's cruelty was legendary, and Frank
      A. Martin who for eight years served as engineer-in-
      chief successively under the *amirs* Abdur Rahman and
      Habibullah, has in his book (1907) devoted full two
      chapters (IX and X) to a painful description of the
      Afghan prisons and executions in use during Abdur
      Rahman's reign. Reading those, one can well appre-
      ciate the description by the Hadda Mulla, Najm al-Din,
      of Amir Abdur Rahman "as one of the most oppressive
      rulers who was hated by the people of Afghanistan"
      (quoted from Kakar 1979, p. 156).

48)   This is the argumentation of the Amir himself, ac-
      cording to Mahomed (1900, II, p. 205).

49)   Amir Abdur Rahman in many ways expressed his belief
      that he as a ruler was especially selected by the
      Almighty and endowed with special qualifications.
      In his autobiography this appears from the revela-
      tions he received. Lord Curzon, who spent several
      months as guest of the Amir also states that the
      Amir "was convinced that he possessed supernatural
      gifts" (Curzon 1923, p. 50).

50)   Peters (1979, pp. 124-135) writes, that in modern
      literature on *jihad* the defensive aspects of *jihad*
      is underlined in the sense that *jihad* outside Isla-
      mic territory is only permitted when the peaceful
      propagation of Islam is being hindered or when Mus-
      lims living amongst unbelievers are oppressed. This
      modernist, defensive tendency originated in India
      in the latter half of the nineteenth century, one of
      the first spokesmen being Sayyid Ahmad Khan. How-
      ever, it should be stressed that Abdur Rahman does
      not belong within this tradition, where *jihad* could
      only be evoked towards religious oppression and a
      separation between the religious and political sphe-
      res were introduced. Rather, Abdur Rahman's ideas
      of *jihad* seems much closer to the ideas of defensive
      jihad current in the Middle East, and particularly
      in Egypt, at that time, in the works of Mohammad
      Abduh and Mohammad Rashid Rida. They asserted that
      the *jihad* duty also applied in case of foreign ag-
      gressor invaded Islamic territory for political and
      economic reasons. Hence, they could appeal to the
      doctrine of *jihad* in order to resist colonial con-
      quest - exactly, what Amir Abdur Rahman did.

51)   For an account of the development of the Afghan
      army, see Kakar (1979, Chapter V).

52)   See for example W.L. Richter, in M. Ayoob (ed.):
      The politics of Islamic Reassertion, 1982.

References:

Adamec, L.W.   : Afghanistan 1900-1923. A Diplomatic
1967   History. Berkeley 1967.

Ahmed, A.S.   : Pukhtun Economy and Society.
1980   Traditional Structure and Economic
                     Development in a Tribal Society.
                     London 1980.

Ayoob, M.   : The Politics of Islamic Reassertion.
1981   London 1981.

Barth, F. (ed.)   : Ethnic Groups and Boundaries.
1969   London 1969.

Bellew, H.W.   : Journal of a Political Mission to
1862   Afghanistan in 1857, with an Account of
                     the country and the People. London 1862.

Bellew, H.W.   : A General Report on the Yusufzais,
1864/77   Lahore (1864)/1977.

Burnes   : Travels into Bokhara, Together with a
1834/1975   Narrative of a Voyage on the Indus,
                     Vol I-III, London. Reprinted Karachi 1975.

Canfield, R.L.   : Faction and Conversion in a Plural Society.
1973   Ann Arbor 1973.

Curzon, Lord of   : Tales of Travel. London 1923.
Keddleston,
1923

Dupree, L.   : The Political Uses of Religion.
1967   In K.H. Silvert (ed): Churches and States:
                     The Religious Institution and Moderniza-
                     tion. New York 1967.

Dupree, L.   : Afghanistan. Princeton 1973.
1973

Einzman, H.   : Religiöse Volksbrauchtum in Afghanistan.
1977   Islamische Heiligenverehrung und
                     Wallfahrtswesen in Raum Kabul.
                     Wiesbaden 1977.

Elphinstone, M.   : An Account of the Kingdom of Caubul, I-II.
1839/1972   Third Edition, London 1839.
                     Reprinted Karachi 1972.

Fairchild, H.P. : Dictionary of Sociology,
1944   Philosophical Library, New York 1944.

Ferrier, J.   : Caravan Journeys and Wanderings in
1857   Persia, Afghanistan, Turkistan and
                  Baluchistan. London 1857.

Ghani, A.   : State-Building and Centralization in a
1977   Tribal Society. Afghanistan 1880-1901.
                  MA-Thesis American University of Beirut
                  (unpublished).

Ghani, A.   : Islam and State-Building in a Tribal
1978   Society. Afghanistan 1880-1901.
                  Modern Asian Studies. Vol. 12, no. 2,
                  pp. 269-284. 1978.

Ghose, D.   : England and Afghanistan: A Phase in
1960   Their Relations. Calcutta 1960.

Gregorian, V.   : The Emergence of Modern Afghanistan.
1969   Politics of Reform and Modernization,
                  1880-1946. Stanford 1969.

Hamilton, A.   : Afghanistan. London 1906.
1906

Kakar, M.H.   : Afghanistan. A Study in Internal
1971   Political Developments, 1880-1896.
                  Kabul 1971.

Kakar, M.H.   : Government and Society in Afghanistan.
1979   The Reign of Amir 'Abd al-Rahman Khan.
                  Austin 1979.

Kaye, J.W.   : History of the War in Afghanistan.
1851   Vol. I-II. London 1851.

Keddie, N.R.   : Sayyid Jamal ad-Din "al-Afghani".
1972   Berkeley 1972.

Kopecky, L-M.   : The Imami Sayyed of the Hazarajat:
1982   The Maintenance of their Social Elite
                  Position. FOLK. Vol. 24. København 1982.

Laclau, E.   : Politics and Ideology in Marxist Theory.
1977   London 1977.

Mahomed, Mir   : The Life of Abdur Rahman, Amir of
Munshi   Afghanistan. Vol. I-II. London 1900.
1900

Martin, F.A.   : Under the Absolute Amir.
1907   London 1907.

Masson, C.   : Narrative of Various Journeys in
1842/1974   Baluchistan, Afghanistan and the
                        Punjab. Vol. I-III. London (1842)/1974.

Mohammad, F.   : Seraj-ul-Tawarikh.   Vol. I-III.
1913-15   Kabul 1913-15.

Muslehuddin, M.   : Sociology and Islam.   Lahore 1977.
1977

Oesterdiekhoff, P.   : Hemnisse und Widersprüche in der
1978   Entwicklung armer Länder.
                        Darstellung am Beispiel Afghanistans.
                        München 1978.

Peters, R.   : Islam and Colonialism.   The Doctrine
1979   of Jihad in Modern History.
                        The Hague 1979.

Poullada, L.B.   : The Pushtun Role in the Afghan Political
1970   System.   Occasional Paper 1.
                        The Afghanistan Council of the Asia
                        Society 1970.

Raverty, M.G.   : Notes on Afghanistan and Parts of
1888/1976   Baluchistan, Geographical, Ethnographi-
                        cal, and Historical.   London 1888.
                        Reprinted Quetta 1976.

Richter, W.L.   : Pakistan.   In M. Ayoob, 1982.
1982

Rodinson, M.   : Marxism and the Muslim World.
1979   London 1979.

Sirat, A.S.   : Sharia and Islamic Education in Modern
1969   Afghanistan.   Middle East Journal.
                        Vol. 23, no. 2, Spring 1969.

Spain, J.W.   : The Pathan Borderland.   The Hague 1963.
1963

Tate, G.P.   : The Kingdom of Afghanistan.
1911/1973   A Historical Sketch.
                        Reprinted Karachi 1973.

Utas, B.   : Notes on Afghan Sufi Orders and
1980   Khanaqahs.   In Afghanistan Journal, Jg.7,
                        Heft 2.   Graz 1980.

Vambery, A.   : Sketches of Central Asia.
  1868/1971   Add. Chapters on My Travels, Ad-
                     ventures and on the Ethnology of
                     Central Asia. London 1868.
                     Reprinted Taipei 1971.

Warburton, R.   : Eighteen Years in Khyber, 1879-1898.
  1900   Reprinted Oxford 1975.

Wilber, D.   : The Structure and Position of Islam
  1952   in Afghanistan. The Middle East
                     Journal. Vol. 6, no. 1. 1952.

Wilber, D.   : Afghanistan. New Haven 1962.
  1962

Yapp, M.E.   : Disturbances in Eastern Afghanistan,
  1962   1839-42. Bulletin of the School of
                     Oriental and African Studies. Vol.25.
                     1962.

ISLAM AND PAKISTAN

by

Frede Højgaard

Pakistan was created as one of the two successor states
to British India, when in 1947 Britain under heavy external
and internal pressure finally gave up ruling that part of
her overseas empire. The carving out of the former British
colony of a separate "homeland for the Muslims of India"
was justified by the Muslim political leadership by a theory that the Indian Muslims constituted a nation separate
from the rest of the Indian people, of whom the vast majority were Hindus. This theory of two nations in India took
definite shape only very late, i.e. when it became politically necessary to use it in the 1930's and 1940's, but in-
timations of Muslim separatism in India can be traced far
back in history. The aim here is to give an outline of the
gradual development of this idea and to attempt to assess
the importance of Islam in its social and political aspects
for the creation of Pakistan.

Islam is a religion which claims to regulate all
aspects of human life, spiritual as well as temporal. This
claim means that social habits and political actions are
not religiously neutral: they are either Islamic or un-
Islamic. The doctrine of Islam is contained in the Quran
and the *sunna* (tradition) of the prophet Muhammad and the
early Muslims. The Quran is considered by the orthodox
Muslim to be the word of God, revealed to the prophet and
authentically transmitted to posterity. The *sunna* has a
somewhat lower status as a source of doctrine, but is nevertheless highly revered. This body of doctrine, however, is
familiar only to a small number of Muslims, in particular
to the religious class known as the *ulama* (the learned men).
The ordinary Muslim will know only fragments of this, but

he will normally have a strong sense of being a Muslim,
that is, of belonging to the community of true believers.
On the social level, therefore, the test of being a Muslim
is not one of knowing the principles of the faith, but one
of a feeling of identity. Such a feeling, naturally, has
political implications: it tends to encourage the idea of
the Muslim community being not only religiously, but also
politically separate from other communities, in accordance
with the basic notion that Islam regulates also that aspect
of life. This at least was the case in the Indian context,
where Islam had been introduced into a very different civilization, that of Hinduism.[1]

The spread of Islam in India was mainly a result, direct or indirect, of conquest. Invasion of India by Muslim
peoples occurred many times between the 8th and the 18th
centuries A.D., and each invasion brought a certain number
of settlers: soldiers, administrators and traders who remained in their new country and usually married there.
Thise people and their descendants became the nucleus of
the Muslim community in India. But the vast majority of
Indian Muslims throughout history were (and are) converts
and their descendants. The first of the conquering generals,
Muhammad bin Qasim, who led an Arab army into Sind in the
early 8th century A.D., followed the by then well-establish-
ed Islamic policy of extending protection to the subjugated
people in return for a poll tax. This he did after having
obtained a ruling on the matter from the *ulama* of Damascus
(Rizvi 1977, p. 14). Many of the native administrators were allowed to continue to function and to
serve as intermediaries between the new ruling class and
the native people, of whom the majority were peasants, but
there was a strong pressure on them to convert to Islam,
and many did so. By conversion, of course, the paying of
the poll tax was no longer required, and this was one important incentive, but there was also an element of coercion
(Rizvi 1977, p. 15; Titus 1959 (1930), pp. 10-11). By the

standards of the time, however, and compared to that of the
later Turkish invaders, Muhammad bin Qasim's policy of conversion was a mild one.

The major incursions of the Middle Ages, which brought
a large part of northern and central India under Muslim
rule, were Turkish, not Arab as that of Sind. The first
wave came around A.D. 1000 under the leadership of a
Turkish Muslim prince, Mahmud of Ghazni. During his reign
he carried out a large number of raids into the Punjab from
his Afghanistan base of Ghazni, and he seems to have been
more concerned to destroy Hindu temples and to carry home
loot than to establish an ordered administration of the
parts of India that his armies overran. However, he ordered missionaries to preach and mosques to be erected in the
conquered territories, and there were also many attempts to
convert large numbers of people by force (Rizvi 1977, pp.
16-17). Such forced conversions were usually ephemeral,
but of lasting impact was the work of the preachers and also the establishment of permanent military garrisons in
Lahore and other towns in the Punjab. During the reign of
the Ghaznavid dynasty in the area a number of Afghan, Iranian and Arabian administrators and scholars settled in the
Ghaznavid dominions, thus further strengthening the Muslim
community there (Hardy 1972, p. 4).

The second great wave of Turkish invasions began in
the late 12th century. The armies of Muhammad Ghori overran the Ghaznavid kingdom in the Punjab and in 1192 defeated
the army of the Hindu Rajput Confederacy, a victory which
laid open the whole of Hindustan for the invaders. During
the following years the whole of the Ganges valley including Bengal was conquered, and previously also Sind
had been secured by Muhammad. In 1206, after Muhammad had
been assassinated in Afghanistan, one of his generals,
Qutb-ud-Din Aibak, established himself as Sultan of Delhi
with effective control of all the Indian conquests (Smith
1958, pp. 235-37). From now on there was a Muslim sovereign
in Delhi (or Agra) until 1858).

Also Muhammad Ghori and his immediate successors showed much zeal in propagating Islam and eradicating idol-worship. Again, there were attempts at forced conversions, no doubt with as little success as previously (Titus 1959, pp. 12-13). However, the Sultans of Delhi very soon came to realize that such methods were counter-productive in political terms. Since they wanted to establish a permanent empire and since it was not possible in a short time to convert the conquered people, they had to adopt a more conciliatory policy and to develop methods for administering their new empire. To this end a significant number of administrators and scholars were brought from the western Muslim lands to India where they settled in the towns of the Jumna-Ganges valley. This immigration, together with the earlier one of a similar kind, became the foundation of Muslim civilization in Hindustan.

A parallel to the attitudes of the Muslim invaders of India may be found in the period of the early European expansion in the late Middle Ages. The Portuguese explorer, Prince Henry (1394-1460), thought it important to convert the heathen, and he saw nothing wrong in depriving non-Christians of their earthly possessions (Parry 1966, pp. 26-27). Such behaviour was also prominent in the initial stages of the Muslim conquests of India, but it should be pointed out that these methods ceased after the consolidation of Muslim power. The religious zeal of Muslims, however, did not slacken but took other forms, mainly that of propagating the faith by preaching, and Islam proved to be very resilient vis-à-vis Hindu civilization in the midst of which it was now implanted. Earlier invaders, such as the Sakas (2nd century B.C.), the Huns (5th century A.D.) and many others, were absorbed within a few generations by that system of social stratification we knwo as the caste system (Smith 1958, p. 266), while the Muslims showed sufficient strength to maintain their identity. In this they were helped by their belief in a definite revelation in time, and in India this belief was undoubtedly strengthened by the observation of the worship of idols by the Hindus, a

practice which Islamic doctrine so heartily condemned. Also
the existence of a geographical centre of Islam, i.e. Mecca,
and of a class of religious scholars (*ulama*) whose task it
was to interpret doctrine to both rulers and the community
of believers in general served to uphold the Muslim sense
of identity.

The introduction of Islam into India thus took place
under violent circumstances. As mentioned above there were
attempts at converting a number of people by force, but with
little success. As soon as the immediate threat of the use
of force disappeared, such converts would revert to their
old religion, and in view of the large number of people who
now came under Muslim rule, forced conversions were relatively insignificant, however gruesome each single incident
may have been. A number of people converted for purely
practical reasons, mainly because it was usually a pre-con-
dition for obtaining posts in the administration, or for
joining the army. But the vast majority of the Indian
Muslims were converted by missionaries. Here members of
the various Sufi orders played a great role. The Sufis
were (and are) brotherhoods of Islamic mystics, usually in
opposition to the official aspect of Islam represented by
the *ulama*. The Sufi missionaries usually settled in villages and gained their adherents by preaching and by their
reputation as saints. The egalitarian nature of Islam and
its rejection (in principle, at least) of caste distinctions
were characteristics which especially attracted low-caste
groups and untouchables. Often whole communities converted
at once. One example of this is the Khojas, a trading community from Gujarat to which M.A. Jinnah belonged (Mujeeb
1967, p. 22).

When the British began to penetrate India in the 18th
century there was a widely dispersed and variegated Muslim
community in the Indian sub-continent. The majority of the
Muslims lived in a broad belt across the northern part of
the country from the borders of Afghanistan and Iran in the
west to Bengal in the east, but there were also a consider-

able number in the Deccan. The first British censuses in
the 1870's and 1880's showed that they were in a majority
in the west, i.e. in Sind and the Punjab and their tribal
borderlands, and in the eastern districts of Bengal, while
in the area in between, which was in fact the heartland of
the Muslim empires, the Muslims were rather fewer, thus in
Agra and Oudh (now Uttar Pradesh) only about 15 per cent of
the total population (Hardy 1972, pp. 4-7). This distribution of Muslims became the basis for the geographical shape
of Pakistan when it was established in 1947 .

The Muslim princes in India may not always have followed the Islamic precepts very strictly, but for the Muslim
community in general the political situation was satisfac-
tory as long as they lived under Muslim rule. There was
therefore no need to express any political "separatism";
the separateness of the Muslims was an integral part of the
political order. When however Muslim rule began to disin-
tegrate in the 18th century, politically conscious Muslims
soon realized that their community was in danger of becoming
subject to Hindu rule. The decline of Mughal power began
after the death of the emperor Aurangzeb in 1707. Wars of
succession weakened the authority at the centre to such an
extent that the centrifugal tendencies, which Aurangzeb had
succeeded in holding in check through a vigorous policy of
military campaigns, were now able to assert themselves.
Provinces such as Bengal in the east and Mysore and
Hyderabad in the south became virtually independent prin-
cipalities, and non-Muslim peoples like the Sikhs and the
Marathas in the west rose in arms against their imperial
masters and threatened the capital itself. The situation of
near-anarchy was further worsened by foreign intrusion. In
1739 the Shah of Persia led an army into North India for
the sake of plunder only. Delhi was thoroughly looted,
and many people were killed.
        For the Muslim community the situation was extremely
worrying. The ideal of an ordered polity based on Islamic

principles was now further from reality than at any time
for centuries. Many orthodox Muslims believed that the decline of Muslim power was caused by luxurious living among
the ruling class. The best known of these, Ahmad ibn Abdul
Rahim, known as Shah Waliullah of Delhi, expressed this view
in a large number of pamphlets and letters and further claimed that the remedy was a return to the pure Islamic precepts
which governed the lives of Muslims at the time of the Prophet and the first four Caliphs (uz-Zaman 1975, p. 78).
However, the military occupation of Delhi by
the Marathas in 1757 made him realize that more immediate
remedies were necessary if Islam in India was to be saved.
He wrote a letter to Ahmad Shah Abdali, the king of Afghanistan, and implored him to come to the rescue of the Indian
Muslims, since "...you are the only King who is powerful,
far-sighted and capable of defeating the enemy forces.
...If, God forbid, domination by infidels continues, Muslims will forget Islam and within a short time become such
a nation that there will be nothing left to distinguish them
from non-Muslims." (Nizami (ed.) 1951, p. 106, quoted in
Sayeed 1968, p. 4). It is a matter of conjecture whether
this letter was in any way instrumental in Ahmad Shah
Abdali's decision to march against the Marathas, when he
did so in 1761; the significant point here is that it shows
his anguish at the prospect of Muslims becoming politically
powerless and even indistinguishable from non-Muslims, a
clear demonstration of his sense of Muslim separateness in
political and religious terms.

The Afghans defeated the Marathas, as Shah Waliullah
had hoped, but they did not have the power to restore
Muslim rule in India. There was no money to pay the Afghan
army, and it had to be withdrawn. The Mughal court linger-
ed on but had no power outside the city of Delhi, and most
of western and central India continued to be in the hands
of the Marathas. The Sikhs were slowly consolidating their
power in the Punjab, and the British East India Company -
who had long had trading stations on the coast - virtually

ruled Bengal since the 1750's and also controlled Madras
and Bombay. The Mughal empire had practically ceased to
function, although theoretically it existed until 1858.
The major contenders for the succession to Mughal power
were the British and the Marathas, and in the struggle between them, which was played out in the first two decades
of the 19th century, the British came out victorious. By
1818 they controlled the Indian subcontinent as far to the
north-west as the borders of the Punjab. Legally, however,
the East India Company was still a vassal of the Mughal emperor in Delhi, a position the Company acknowledged by following the custom of paying a yearly tribute to the emperor.
Such an act was generally understood in India as being a
symbol of allegiance (Buckler 1966, pp. 46 - 51).
This situation of *de jure* suzerainty of the Mughal emperor
gave an appearance of India still being under Muslim rule,
but where the real power lay was not in doubt. The well-
known poet Ghalib, who had been a protegé of the Mughal
court, in 1856 decided to shift *his* allegiance and wrote a
Persian ode to Queen Victoria which he sent to the British
Governor-General Lord Canning and asked him to forward it
to London (Russell and Khurshidul Islam 1969, p. 130).
Most Muslims must have come to a similar conclusion about
the power relations, although few reacted in this somewhat
less than dignified manner.

During the third and fourth decades of the 19th century
the British made use of their powerful position to conduct
a vigorous policy of modernization within their domains.
Many of the British innovations were deeply resented by
educated Muslims. The two decrees which concerned them
most were the introduction of Western education in 1835 and
the replacement of Persian by English as an administrative
and court language in 1837. Muslim civilization in India
was closely bound up with Persian, and in material terms
the change meant that a large number of Muslims in official
employment lost their jobs, since they were unfamiliar with
English. In this field Muslims had outnumbered Hindus

because of their knowledge of Persian. The Muslim community
as a whole was very reluctant to take up the study of English
because it was felt as an abandonment of their own culture
and even as a danger to their religion. There was at the
same time a strong missionary activity going on under British
protection, and many Muslims feared that the language policy
was part of a scheme to convert their community. The hostility which this created among educated Muslims spread widely
in the community; many Muslims felt that India was no longer
an Islamic country, and some even advocated emigration
(Singhal 1972, pp. 38-39). This anti-British sentiment among
the Indian Muslims was one of the major causes of the great
rebellion of 1857-58 which is known under the name of the
Mutiny, but it cannot be called Indian nationalism, and not
even Muslim nationalism. It was a result of Muslim interests
being harmed and Muslim pride being hurt by British highhand-
edness. The hope of the Muslims was not to create a national
state but to restore the Mughal empire, as events during the
Mutiny showed.

The Mutiny in 1857-58 - by Indian and Pakistani historians often called the First War of Independence - was not a
wholly Muslim affair, however. It started as a proper mutiny in Meerut in May 1857 among the regiments of the so-called
Bengal Army, which was recruited by the East India Company,
initially in Bengal - hence its name - but later mainly in
the North-Western Provinces, i.e. the area which is today
the Uttar Pradesh. As soon as the mutiny in Meerut had succeeded, the soldiers, even without proper leadership, almost as if by instinct, marched on Delhi, the old capital of
the Mughal empire, where they persuaded the eighty-two year
old Bahadur Shah, the last of the Mughal emperors, to assume
the official leadership of the revolt. Soon the revolt
spread into the countryside, first into Muslim villages
south and south-east of Delhi, which rose as if by command.
There is no direct evidence, however, that their rebellion
had been planned beforehand. Later also Hindu areas rose

against the British; in fact, most of the civil risings were
led by Hindus. Among the Muslims, leadership was often assumed by members of the religious class, many of whom had
even before the rebellion expressed the view that India under British rule was no longer fit for Muslims to live in
(Hardy 1972, pp. 62 ff).

Outside northern and central India, the main area of
rebellion, Muslims were generally quiet. Most Muslim civil
servants actively supported them. One of these was Sir
Sayyid Ahmad Khan, the famous educationalist, who, being a
magistrate in Company service, made an attempt to pacify his
district. In spite of the fact that the Muslims were by no
means united against them, the British took the view that
the rebellion was mainly of Muslim doing, an attitude the
cause of which may be found in the attempt of the mutineers
to restore the Mughal empire, in the rapid spread of the
rebellion to Muslim villages, and in the fact that many Muslim religious men emerged as leaders of local revolts. After the rebellion had been quelled, the British took their
revenge and feelings ran high. The British Prime Minister,
Palmerston, even ordered the Governor-General to have every
Muslim building demolished "without regard to antiquarian
veneration or artistic prediliction." (Quoted in Hardy 1972,
p. 71). However, the Governor-General and his advisers
adopted the wiser policy of reconciliation; no symbols of
Muslim civilization were destroyed as a matter of deliberate
policy, and soon the military vengeance was brought under
control. The British victory, however, was a stunning blow
to the Muslim community. The last symbol of Muslim rule in
India, the Mughal empire, was finally abolished in 1858, and
the uncontrolled British rage in the period immediately after the end of the fighting created much bitterness among
the Muslims.

The Muslim reaction to the British victory took, broad-
ly speaking, three forms. The anti-British movement which
had existed before the rebellion became more violent and

sought to continue the fight against the foreigners by military means. Others who had been in the same movement realized that the military cause was lost with the failure of the rebellion and turned to education with the aim of preserving Islam in its purity. Finally there was a section of the Muslims under the leadership of Sir Sayyid Ahmad Khan,the Magistrate, who also realized that Muslim power was broken, but who believed that the only way to preserve Islam in India was to adjust to modern western ideas and to support British imperial power.

The violent movement succeeded in creating a number of disturbances in northern India in the years following the rebellion. It was led by militant Muslim divines who considered India to be *dar al-harb* (land of war), an opinion which had been expressed as early as 1803 by the son of Shah Waliullah (Singhal 1972, p. 41). In Islamic law the existence of *dar al-harb* demands *jihad*, or struggle, if necessary armed struggle, to turn the area in question into *dar al-islam*. Another legal reaction to this situation may be emigration, and as the attempts at revolt regularly failed, many of the militants migrated to the tribal area on the North-West Frontier, beyond British jurisdiction, where they set up a colony which maintained itself well into the 20th century despite military efforts to dislodge them. The movement showed the extreme of the Muslim sense of separateness, but it had no real practical results and was in fact more of an embarrassment to than a support for the Muslim community as a whole.

The less militant, but still anti-British, Muslim element turned to the study and teaching of their faith. In 1867 they established an Islamic school at Deoband in North India. The aim of this school was to teach the *sharia* (the holy law of Islam) as the basis of an intended missionary activity. The missionary activity was aimed more at restoring and purifying the faith than actually spreading it. The students were trained to act as teachers of Islamic theology in other institutions of learning, as private tutors and as prayer-leaders in Muslim congregations (Mujeeb 1967, p. 522). The Deoband movement did not consider India to be *dar al-harb*; they accepted decrees by Indian and Arabian divines that as long as certain Islamic institutions were allowed to exist, even under a non-Muslim government, India was still legally *dar al-islam* (Hunter 1969 (1871), pp. 207-209). However, they considered British rule to be an anomaly in which they only acquiesced because it was too powerful to get rid of.

In contrast to the orthodox Deoband movement, the movement led by Sir Sayyid Ahmad Khan not only accepted British rule but positively supported it. Sir Sayyid saw the British as the guarantors of the religious freedom of the Muslims in India and maintained that Christianity and Islam were so alike that there could be no objection to Muslims being ruled by a Christian government. He wrote copiously to spread his ideas and from the 1870's onwards published an Urdu journal which became very popular. In a long commentary on the *Quran* he argued that the principles of Islam could not be contrary to modern scientific notions, even though these were developed in the West, since the word of God could not be in conflict with nature, the creation of God. He encouraged Muslims to take up the study of the English language, the knowledge of which would allow them to participate in public life, and also to study modern western works in all branches of learning. His attitude to the Hindus was one of tolerance, and he even argued that Muslims ought to abstain from cow-slaughter so as not to offend pious Hindus (Sayeed 1968, p. 18). Yet he also once wrote about the Hindus and the Muslims as two different nations, and this is believed to be the first instance of this modern notion of the Muslims of India as a nation being used (Singhal 1972, p. 43). This sense of a difference between Hindus and Muslims developed as a response to the establishment of the Indian National Congress in 1885. The prospect of one national organisation representing both communities looked ominous to him, since Muslims would always be in a minority

and consequently would be unable to protect their interests
(Hardy 1972, p. 130).

Sir Sayyid also took great interest in education. After
the great rebellion had been quelled, it was inevitable that
the British policy of using English as the medium of both
administration and higher education should be continued, and
Sir Sayyid not only accepted this but actively supported it.
At the same time he worked for the improvement of Urdu by
encouraging the translation of modern scientific works into
that language. In 1864 he founded a Scientific Society
mainly for this purpose. During a visit to Britain in 1869-
70 he worked out a plan for the establishment of a university college which should work along the same lines, and only
a few years later the plan was put into practice in the
shape of the Anglo-Muhammadan Oriental College at Aligarh,
ordinary school classes starting in 1875 and classes at college level in 1878. The College was open to students of all
beliefs, and it regularly had a fair number of Hindu students, although it was meant primarily for Muslims. The
college took the British public school as its model and consequently placed the emphasis on developing such qualities
as leadership, character and physical prowess rather than
intellectual excellence. Although Islamic theology (both
sunni and shii) was part of the curriculum, Islam was mainly
considered to be a cultural rather than a religious concept
(Ahmad 1967, pp. 36-38; Hardy 1972, pp. 103 f). With its
wholly pragmatic and modernizing outlook the college came
to play an important role in the development of the idea of
Pakistan.

In the decades after the rebellion of 1857-58 it was
British policy to guarantee the right of the various religious communities to practice their religions in peace.
This policy encouraged a political way of thinking within
these communities when they felt they had to take action to
counter infringements, real or imagined, of that right.
Also the growing need on the part of the government for

administrative staff (at the lower levels) tended to increase political consciousness in the communities, since an
element of competition was evident in the filling of administrative posts (Hardy 1972, pp. 116 f). A number of associ-
ations for the promotion of Muslim culture came into being
in this period, and their work further strengthened the
feeling of Muslim identity.

The establishment of the Indian National Congress in
1885 forced leading Muslims to take up in earnest the
question of the political future of the Muslims in India under British rule. A well-known Muslim leader in Bombay,
Badruddin Tyabji, advocated Muslim participation in the Congress and, in general, Muslim co-operation with their fel-
low-countrymen of other communities, for in this way to "advance the general progress of India and at the same time
safeguard our own interests." (Quoted in Hardy 1972, p. 129).
It was this idea of close co-operation with other communities, in particular the Hindus, that Sir Sayyid was so strongly against. In the end Sir Sayyid's viewpoint won, which
was demonstrated by the establishment of the Muslim League
in 1906.

The early years of the 20th century were a period of
great political ferment in India. In the Punjab the provincial government decided to reserve 30 per cent of all positions in the civil service for Muslims. This measure was
an attempt to prevent the Muslims falling behind the Hindus
among whom there were a larger proportion of people with
higher education. The Muslims, however, felt this to be an
injustice, since their community constituted more than 50
per cent of the population. furthermore, the Hindus dominated the great municipalities of the province, and had
done so since the introduction of the elective principle in
the early 1880's, because urban Hindus were generally speaking wealthier and better educated than urban Muslims. On
the other hand the Muslim community in the Punjab benefitted
from another government measure, the Land Alienation Act
of 1901, which was designed to protect the small peasant

proprietors against moneylenders. As the Muslim majority
was more pronounced in the countryside than in the towns,
and as the moneylenders were usually Hindus, the Act was
felt to be in favour of the Muslim community (Hardy 1972,
p. 152). Because of this and also because the Punjabis
traditionally tended to look inwards for political solutions, Punjabi Muslims were rather less inclined to take
political action on an all-India basis than were their fel-
low Muslims of the United Provinces, the traditional heartland of the Mughal empire. This tendency to perceive politics in Punjabi rather than all-India terms in fact persist-
ed right until the end of the Second World War.

In Bengal public opinion was much excited by the partition of the province in 1905. This measure was introduced
mainly for the sake of making the administration easier; before the partition the province had a population of over 78
million, as much as France and Great Britain together. The
new boundary came to divide the old province almost along
religious lines, so that the eastern part became a new province with a very large Muslim majority. The government
must have been aware of this, but it was not aware of the
consequences which followed. Led by western-educated Bengali intellectuals agitation against the partition spread
all over Bengal, and at first both Hindus and Muslims joined
in, which was a manifestation of a fairly strong Bengali nationalism. But the new Muslim majority province soon offer-
ed new opportunities for Bengali Muslims, and Muslim feeling
began to move towards support for the new state of things.
Hindu agitation, on the contrary, increased in strength, and
in 1911 the Government decided to re-unite the province. The
whole affair had tended to alienate both communities from
the Government, since it had given both cause for mistrust,
and it had strongly enhanced political consciousness, not
least among the Muslims.

In the United Provinces educated Muslim opinion had
long followed the lead of Sayyid Ahmad Khan. By the early
20th century, however, a new element had emerged which

questioned the Sayyid's confidence in British rule. The
split had been occasioned by an argument about the use of
Urdu or Hindi in the lower law courts. Urdu had been used
exclusively, but a movement for the alternative use of Hindi
had succeeded in persuading the Lieutenant Governor of the
province to allow the courts to choose between the two langu-
ages (scripts) and to demand of court officials a knowledge
of both scripts. There was a strong Muslim reaction to this
as it was felt to be an attack on Muslim culture (Hardy 1972,
p. 143). The leaders of this new element were mostly pro-
fessional men of the younger generation, often lawyers and
often of landowning families. Two of them were Muhammad Ali
and his brother Shaukat Ali who both became famous as Muslim leaders during the Khilafat agitation after the First
World War. The older, conservative Muslims were uneasy a-
bout the new radicals, and there was an attempt to found a
political association in the United Provinces under conservative leadership, probably with the aim of countering the
radicals. It came to nothing, however (Hardy 1972, p. 153).
Common to the Muslims of the United Provinces was a less
narrow, a more all-Indian outlook than that found in either
the Punjab or Bengal, a legacy of the Muslim empires which
had their centres there. There was also among the Muslims
of the United Provinces a higher awareness of the general
situation of the Indian Muslims, that of being in a minority
vis-à-vis the Hindu majority. In the United Provinces Muslims were spread thinly among the Hindus, whereas in the
Punjab and Bengal there were areas with solid Muslim majori-
ties. On the other hand, in the United Provinces a higher
proportion of the Muslims lived in towns and cities and were
better off and better educated than elsewhere.

On account of all this the political atmosphere was
tense, and the British thought certain measures necessary to
calm the situation. In July 1906 the Secretary of State for
India, John Morley, a member of the newly elected Liberal
government of Britain, announced in the House of Commons

that he was in favour of political reforms in India giving
representatives of Indian interests a greater say in the
Viceroy's and the Governors' executive councils as well as
in the legislative councils. Before this announcement he
had had talks with the moderate Congress leader G.K. Gokhale,
and the announcement was clearly an attempt to win over moderate Indian opinion to the side of Government. This new
British policy rekindled the old fear of educated Muslim
opinion which had first been expressed by Sayyid Ahmad Khan
that Muslim interests would suffer under any form of repre-
sentative government because of the general majority of
Hindus, and it was in fact the more conservative element,
which may largely be said to be followers of the Sayyid,
that reacted. The Viceroy, Lord Minto was approached, and
on the 1st of Ocotber 1906 he received a deputation of Muslim representatives from all Indian provinces except the
North-West Frontier Province.

The initiative to the meeting was taken by the Secretary of the Aligarh College, and the delegation was led by the
Agha Khan, the wealthy and influential leader of the Muslim
community known as the Ismailis. The delegation presented
an address signed by "nobles, ministers of various states,
great landowners, lawyers, merchants, and many other of His
Majesty's Mahommedan subjects." (Sayeed 1968, p. 28). The
address expressed the wish for separate representation of
Muslims in all councils: municipalities, district boards
and provincial and central legislative councils. In reply
the Viceroy declared that he was fully in agreement with the
principles of the address but for the time being reserved
his opinion as to how exactly these principles should be put
into practice (Sayeed 1968, p. 28; Hardy 1972, p. 154).

The benevolent attitude of the British towards the Muslim community was reciprocated a few months later by the
founding of the All-India Muslim League. The meeing at
which the League was established was convened on the 30th
of December 1906 at Dacca in eastern Bengal which was very
natural in view of the fact that there the Muslim community

had experienced a renewal of political life as a result of
the partition in the previous year. The main draughtsman
of the League constitution was Maulana Muhammad Ali, one of
the spokesmen of the younger, radical section of the Muslims
of the United Provinces, but even so the conservative followers of Sayyid Ahmad Khan were the more influential. The
first resolution of the League laid down its aims: (1) to
foster loyalty among the Muslims of India towards the British;
(2) to work for the political interests of Muslims; to im-
prove relations between the Muslims and the other communities
of India (Sayeed 1968, p. 30). This was a programme quite
in keeping with the interests of those sections of the Muslims which stood behind the League, the same people who had
signed the address to the Viceroy in October. The man who
later became the unchallenged leader of the League and the
chief architect of Pakistan, Muhammad Ali Jinnah, was not
involved in the foundation of the League; at the time he was
a secretary to the president of the Indian National Congress
and a strong opponent of the League (Singhal 1972,p. 49).

The understanding between the Muslims and the British
was expressed in political terms in the constitutional reforms which were introduced in 1909 by a British Act of
Parliament. The reforms were an accept of the Muslim demands put forward in the address to the Viceroy in 1906.
The Muslims were given the right to elect Muslim representatives by separate electorates, and in addition to that, the
right also to vote in the general constituencies. Furthermore, they were accorded weightage in representation in some
areas, i.e. the number of seats reserved for Muslim candidates were higher than their proportion of the population
would normally warrant (Sayeed 1968, pp. 30-31). These concessions may, in retrospect, be said to be the first real
step towards the establishment of a Muslim state in the
Indian sub-continent, although such a thing was not seriously contemplated by anyone at the time. The Muslims guarded
these rights jealously and succeeded in retaining them in
spite of criticism from the National Congress, the crucial

point being, of course, the British interest in upholding them.

The honeymoon between the British and the Muslims did not last, however. The reunification of Bengal in 1911 was felt by the Muslim League as a betrayal of trust, and the more radical section of the Muslims began to gain influence in the League. The British declaration of war against Turkey in 1914 furthered this tendency towards radicalism. In 1915 Muhammad Ali Jinnah, who had become a member of the League in 1913 and rapidly gained a strong influence in it, managed together with his supporters to persuade both the Congress and the League to hold their annual sessions in Bombay, thereby initiating negotiations between the two organisations which led to an agreement between them. The agreement, known as the Lucknow Pact, was entered into in 1916, when the two organisations held their annual sessions in Lucknow. The most important point in the Pact was that the Congress accepted the principle of separate electorates for the Muslims, in fact offering an even better representation than was conceded in the reforms of 1909.

The understanding between the two major communities of British India was a natural outcome of the political situation during the war years. Both Muslim League and Congress leaders realized that the strains of war weakened the British vis-à-vis Indian political opinion and that consequently a united political front on the Indian side might succeed in wrenching major concessions from the imperial power. The claim of the Indian nationalists was for Home Rule (a parallel to the simultaneous Irish claim), but this demand was not fulfilled. Most of the constitutional elements contained in the Lucknow Pact was incorporated in the new Government of India Act of 1919, but the substance of Home Rule, viz. that all internal matters should be decided by elected Indian councils, was not conceded; the British reserved for the imperial power the right to decide the crucial matters of finance, internal security and defence and

furthermore the right of the Viceroy and the provincial
governors to overrule any decision by any elected body, if
in their judgment imperial interests demanded it.

The Act of 1919 was a profound disappointment to both
the Muslim League and the Congress, but the reaction of the
two organisations was entirely different. During the popular unrest which followed the end of the war the Congress,
which was captured by M.K. Gandhi and his supporters in
1920, went from strength to strength, whereas the League
practically lost all political influence. Jinnah was a
strong believer in constitutionalism and could not accept
the political methods employed by Gandhi during his non-cooperation movement. Muslim disaffection was channelled into
the Khilafat movement, organised and led by the two brothers
Muhammad and Shaukat Ali from the United Provinces in support of the Caliph who was also the Sultan of Turkey. The
movement was, however, mainly fed by internal grievances
common to Hindus and Muslims: prices rising as a result of
the war, the introduction by the British of stricter measures to deal with unrest, the lack of British generosity
in constitutional matters. The Ali Brothers followed the
lead of Gandhi and participated in the non-cooperation movement, with the declared aim of obtaining Home Rule for India.
But the cooperation between Congress and the Khilafatists
(or "Hindu-Muslim Unity" as the slogan went) could not last.
When Gandhi called off the movement in 1922, it had to be
realized that the common enemy, the British, were practically unshaken, and as a result of the political frustra-
tion which followed, the belief in a common political de-
stiny for the two communities rapidly broke down, and a
series of bloody Hindu-Muslim riots occurred. The period
of Hindu-Muslim unity which began with the Lucknow Pact in
1916 ended by 1924, and such political understanding between
the two communities never occurred again (Sayeed 1968, pp.
42 ff; Hardy 1972, pp. 185 ff).

The Reforms Act of 1919 stipulated that the question of

constitutional reform should be taken up again within ten
years, and in 1927 the Conservative British government appointed an all-British parliamentary commission to survey
the problem. In defence of the measure to make the commission exclusively British the Secretary of State for India,
Lord Birkenhead, declared that since the Indians could not
agree on a constitution among themselves, constitutional reforms were solely a British responsibility (Hardy 1972, p.
212; Sayeed 1968, p. 69). This challenge was taken up by
Indian political leaders, and an All-Parties Conference was
convened in 1928 to propose an Indian constitution. The
conference empowered its chairman, Motilal Nehru, and its
secretary, his son Jawaharlal Nehru, to draft a proposal.
Their report (the Nehru Report) proposed the abandonment of
the principle of separate electorates, only with a reservation of seats for Muslims in Muslim minority provinces, on
the grounds that normal democratic procedures constituted
sufficient safeguards for Muslims. A section of the Muslim
League rejected the report outright, while another section
under the leadership of Jinnah consented to discuss the proposal at a new All-Parties Convention in December 1928. Here
Jinnah demanded reservation of seats for Muslims in elected
bodies on a population basis in all provinces, as well as
one third of the seats in the Central Legislature. He also
advocated the creation of an Indian Federation with a weak
central government and all residuary powers vested in the
provinces, a measure which would further, as he saw it,
diminish the risk of Hindu majority domination of the Muslims. There was however an overwhelming majority against
all these proposals at the Convention, and Jinnah and his
supporters decided to withdraw. He later published his demands, summarised in fourteen points, which became the political platform of the Muslim League (Hardy 1972, pp. 212-
13; Sayeed 1968, pp. 72-73). This was, so to speak, the seal
on the alienation of the Muslims from the Hindus which had
already become manifest earlier in the decade.
 During the civil disobedience campaign led by Gandhi in

1930 and 31, the Muslim League and most other Muslim grou-
pings kept aloof. Jinnah, the Ali Brothers and other Muslim
leaders participated in the Round Table Conference in London
in 1930, 1931 and 1932, at which the report of the Parliamentary Commission was discussed. Here they became even more
alienated from Gandhi, who, when he participated in the second session of the Conference in 1931, insisted on being
the spokesman for the whole of India. Jinnah became so disillusioned by this experience that he withdrew from politics
altogether and settled in England to practice law. His political defeat followed from the fact that he had no real following among the Muslims; he learnt the lesson that his eminent ability to plead a case was quite insufficient to produce political results, when he did not have the majority of
those on whose behalf he pleaded solidly behind him. When
he returned to Indian politics a few years later, he drew
the consequences of this lesson.

The rejection of the Muslim demands at the All-Parties
Convention forced the Muslim League to reconsider the situation. At the Convention a vague proposal for a separate Muslim state within India had been discussed but was firmly rejected by the majority. Now this idea was taken up in earnest
by the well-known writer and poet Muhammad Iqbal, who during
1930 was the President of the Muslim League. In his presi-
dential address at the League session in Allahabad in December 1930 he formulated a theory of a Muslim state in the
words, "I would like to see the Punjab, North-West Frontier
Province, Sind and Baluchistan amalgamated into a single
State." (Naim (ed.) 1979, p. 195). Such a state should have
selfgovernment but should otherwise remain "within the body
politic of India..." (Naim (ed.) 1979, p. 196). Such a state
(and India as a whole) might, according to Iqbal, remain formally within the British Empire. However, at the time the
idea of a separate Muslim state was considered wholly im-
practicable by the Congress, by the Government and even by
the majority of Muslims, and the Muslim League was so weak
in political terms that its pronouncements were not taken

seriously. So few people attended the 1930 session that it could not pass valid resolutions according to the League's own constitution.

On the other hand, the idea once launched lived on and was taken up by a few Muslims here and there. In 1933 an Indian student at Cambridge University, Chaudhuri Rahmat Ali, published a pamphlet in which he devised a name for a Muslim state in India. From the initial letters in the provinces of Punjab, Afghania (i.e. the North-West Frontier Province), Kashmir, Sind and Baluchistan he derived the word Pakistan, (Ahmad 1967, p. 169; Edib 1937, p. 352), which appealed to him so much the more as the pak in Urdu means 'religiously pure'. Rahmat Ali had no direct contact with political life in India, and his nationalist ideas developed into unrealistic schemes of a "Pakasia", but the name of Pakistan stuck, as we know. However, the second meaning of the word was later repudiated by Jinnah during his negotiations with Gandhi in 1944; Gandhi had objected to the notion of a 'land of the pure' which implied that the rest of India was 'impure', and Jinnah accepted the objection as valid while insisting on retaining the name, since in the mind of Muslims it had become synonymous with the demand for a Muslim homeland (Ahmad 1967, p. 169).

Although the major Indian political association,the Congress, could not participate because it was paralysed by the arrest of its leaders, constitution-making continued on the basis of the results of the Round Table Conference. The proceedings now took place in the British Parliament, and they were marked by the strong opposition by a wing of the Conservatives, led by Winston Churchill, to the granting of Dominion status (i.e. the practical autonomy within the Empire, such as e.g., Canada enjoyed at the time). This was the real stumbling-block for the Congress, and even for those Muslim and other Indian political leaders who chose to co-operate, that the Constitution of their country should be finally decided by a Parliament elected wholly in Britain. The

Round Table Conference ended in 1932, but because of the
delaying tactics of Churchill and his supporters the new
Government of India Act was only passed in 1935. The Act
provided for fully responsible government in the provinces,
i.e. all departments were to be headed by ministers who enjoyed the confidence of an elected Legislative Assembly, and
the Governor was normally to act as a constitutional head
but had in fact the power to dismiss his ministers and dis-
solve the Assembly if he considered it necessary. In the
central government the imperial power reserved for itself
the crucial departments of finance, foreign policy, defence
and judiciary, whereas the other departments were given to
ministers responsible to a central legislative assembly. The
Act also envisaged establishing an Indian Federation of the
provinces and the native states, but this was made dependent
on the willingness of the princes to join in, and they were
very reluctant to do so. Both the Congress and the Muslim
League initially rejected the Act as being wholly unsatis-
factory but later decided to accept it and to contest the
elections which were held under it in the beginning of 1937
(Keith 1969 (1926), pp. 319 ff).

The Muslim League had persuaded Jinnah to return to
India in 1935 to reorganise and lead the League during the
election campaign. He set up a Central Parliamentary Board
with the aim of approving a list of League candidates to
fight a nation-wide campaign with a political programme de-
manding full self-government, measures to relieve the peasants of debts, free primary education and an economic policy to encourage industrial production. This programme was
in fact very similar to that of the Congress. But it proved
very difficult for the League to make the Muslims respond to
its call. Provincial Muslim parties of long standing had
far more powerful organisations than it was possible for
the League to build up in a short time, and the local leaders were reluctant to co-operate with a man like Jinnah
who had no political following of his own and no direct experience of political work under the previous constitution.

Consequently the League was not able to put up candidates
for all the seats reserved for Muslims (Ahmad 1967, p. 165;
Hardy 1972, p. 224).

In the elections the League fared very badly, gaining
only about five per cent of the Muslim vote. The best results were obtained in the United Provinces, in which, as
mentioned earlier, the Muslims were in a minority and therefore felt the risk of Hindu political domination more keen-
ly, but even here independent Muslim candidates won more
seats than the league, thirty as against the League's twen-
ty-four. In Bengal the League won thirty-seven out of 119
Muslim seats. In the west it commanded almost no electoral
support at all, winning only two seats in the Punjab (out of
86 Muslim seats) and in Sind, the North-West Frontier Province and Baluchistan none at all. This was a very dis-
heartening experience for the Muslim League leaders, in particular that it was the Muslim majority areas which showed
the least interest in the League. For the Congress, in contrast, the election was a great success, giving them a clear
majority in six of the eleven provinces and making them the
largest single party in three others (Hardy 1972, pp. 224-
25; Sayeed 1968, pp. 83-84). Jawaharlal Nehru expressed his
interpretation of the election result in the declaration
that "there are only two forces in India today, British imperialism and Indian nationalism as represented by the Congress."
(Brecher 1959, p. 231).

During the election campaign the influential Muslim
Congress-man Maulana Abul Kalam Azad had given the Muslim
League leaders in the United Provinces, Chaudhari Khaliquzzaman and Nawab Ismail Khan the assurance that the Cong-
gress would be willing to enter into a coalition with the
League when the new U.P. Government had to be formed after
the election, giving the two Muslim leaders a ministry each.
However, while Azad was away to help in the negotiations for
a Congress government in Bihar, Nehru, not knowing the details of Azad's promise, informed Khaliquzzaman that the e-
lection result only justified one Muslim League minister in

the U.P. Government (Azad 1959, p. 144). The Congress further demanded that the Muslim minister and the Muslim League
members in the Assembly must accept Congress majority decisions, the very thing the Muslims feared most of all (Hardy
1972, pp. 225-26). It is no wonder that the Muslim League
rejected co-operation with the Congress on these conditions;
acceptance would have meant the death of the League as a
political organisation.

Jinnah now deliberately set out to show that there was
a third force in India to be reckoned with, the Muslims. In
the United Provinces the League leadership in its propaganda
played on the fears of the Muslim landowning class that the
new Congress provincial government would adopt policies de-
trimental to their interests. Such measures were indeed introduced: in 1938 the U.P. Legislature passed a bill which
reduced the lawful rents to about half. The bill was, however, disallowed by the Governor and so did not become law,
but it made Congress intentions clear. Later another bill
was passed which did become law, improving the legal security of tenants. In all Congress-governed provinces new
laws regulating basic education were passed, introducing
Gandhian ideas: booklearning combined with the learning of
handicraft and spinning, and the use of textbooks in Hindi
glorifying Hindu historical and religious heroes (Hardy
1972, p. 227). The Congress Working Committee adopted as
the new national anthem a few stanzas from a poem by the name
of "Bande Mataram" which had first appeared in a violently
anti-Muslim novel, and although the stanzas selected did not
in themselves exhibit any specific anti-Muslim feeling, it
was too much to expect Muslims to accept them as a symbol
of their national feeling (Sayeed 1968, p. 91).

There were other Congress measures which grated on Muslim sensibilities, in particular those of the political leaders. After their election victory the Congress launched a
"mass contact" campaign which emphasized the common economic
and social interests of the common people whether they were
Muslims or Hindus. As the since 1909 existing principle of

separate electorates for Muslims had just been confirmed in
the new Government of India Act of 1935, this Congress campaign was understood by politically conscious Muslims as an
attempt to deprive Muslim politicians of their electoral support. In their own campaign at this time to gain support
Muslim League politicians tried to counteract this. In their
tours of the countryside they met many of the Congress political workers and were confirmed in their belief that Congress was basically a Hindu organisation, despite its claims
to be a non-religious body; the Congress workers were often
men of little understanding of Muslim or European political
thought, speaking in an entirely Hindu idiom (Hardy 1972,
p. 227).

The Muslim League campaign was a success. When the Second World War broke out Jinnah was consulted by the Viceroy
as to how to organise Indian support for the war effort. The
British had always claimed - partly as a justification of
their rule - that there were two conflicting forces in India, the Hindus and the Muslims. This claim looked less obviously true after that the 1937 elections had shown that
there was no real nation-wide representation for the Muslims,
and the Government was now happy to see that the League had
built up so much strength that it could be counted on as a
political force strong enough to be used as a counter-weight
to the Congress. After the Viceroy had declared war on
Germany on behalf of India without consulting the Indian political parties, the Congress reacted by having all Congress
provincial governments resign. In the negotiations which
followed between the Government, the Congress and the League,
Jinnah was able to obtain the concession from the British
that the 1935 Act should be reconsidered and that no constitution should be introduced in India without the consent of
both the major parties, the League and the Congress (Hardy
1972, pp. 229-30).

This was in fact a major political victory for the
League, and the intentions of how to use its newly won influence and status were soon made public. In March 1940, at

its session in Lahore, the League passed what came to be
known as the "Pakistan Resolution", although the work Pakistan
did not occur in it.   The crucial passage went thus,

> "no constitutional plan would be .... acceptable to
> the Muslims unless it is designed on the following
> basic principles, viz., that geographical conti-
> guous units are demarcated into regions which should
> be so constituted .... that the areas in which the
> Muslims are numerically in a majority as in the
> North-Western and Eastern zones of India should be
> grouped to constitute "Independent States" in which
> the constituent units shall be autonomous and so-
> vereign."
>
> (Naim 1979, p. 208)

The notion of an independent Muslim homeland (or homelands)
in India was now the official policy of the Muslim League,
although it was expressed in a somewhat vague and ambiguous
way.   But the League suffered from one major weakness: its
political support was almost entirely confined to areas in
which Muslims were in a minority, i.e., mainly the United
Provinces, whereas in the "North-Western and Eastern zones"
which the resolution envisaged as the Muslim "Independent
States", local Muslim parties distinct from the League were
in control.   Here the two provinces of Bengal and the Punjab
came to play a crucial role, but also the North-West Frontier Province became of some importance.

   In Bengal just over half the population were Muslims,
most of whom lived in the eastern districts of the province.
With the beginning of participation in politics by Indians
in the 1920's a political party arose which represented mainly the peasants and agricultural tenants of the eastern districts.   In the election of 1937 this party, the Krishak
Praja Party, became the largest party in the provincial legislature without, however, having the absolute majority.
The party had earlier had some connection with the Congress,
and after the election in 1937 the party leader, Fazl al-Haq
tried to form a government in coalition with the Congress.
This came to nothing, however, and in the end he sought and
obtained the support of the Muslim League.   It is indicative

of the relative unimportance of the League at that time that
the leader of the Muslim Krishak Praja Party should approach
the Congress first when trying to form a government.

Fazl al-Haq's government was not able to fulfil its pro-
mises of a reduction in taxes and better security for tenants. The landlord interest was well represented in the
party and the British-led administrative system was still
powerful and by tradition inclined to support vested interests. He soon fell out with the League which he accused of
interference in Bengal politics, and he tried to find new
coalition partners, the Hindu Mahasabha, an extreme Hindu
party, in order to remain in power. This alliance could not
last and in 1943 his government fell and was replaced by a
Muslim League government. From now on until the new elections in 1946 a major shift in the allegiance of the Muslim
electorate occurred. Very little is known so far about how
this shift took place, but there is no doubt that the peasants and their local leaders had become disillusioned with
the Krishak Praja Party which had gained practically nothing
for them. The Muslim League in its agitation now held out the
promise of a Pakistan in which there would be justice for all
Muslims; in this they could play on the peasant antagonism
towards the landlords of whom the majority in the otherwise
Muslim districts were Hindus. The wealthy and educated
sections of the Muslims had discovered that there were advantages to be gained from a Muslim government, such as
jobs for the younger generation and official patronage. The
success for the League, in any case, was clear for all to
see: in the provincial election in 1946 it won 113 out of
the 119 Muslim seats.[2]

In the Punjab political life in the 1920's and 1930's
was dominated by the Unionist Party which drew its support
mainly from the landed gentry. The local political factions
were led by landlords, particularly in the western districts;
in the eastern districts there were fewer big landlords, and
here leaders of kinship groups dominated local politics.
These local magnates were partly created by the British and

strongly supported by them through the granting of titles
and posts in the local administration. In return they were
thoroughly loyal to the British, and remained so right until
it became clear towards the end of the Second World War that
British rule was drawing to a close. In 1937 the Unionist
Party won a resounding victory in the provincial election
and formed the government without having to enter into any
coalition. As related above, the Muslim League made a poor
showing in that election, but during the League campaign afterwards Jinnah succeeded in persuading the Unionists to enter into a pact with the League, according to which the Unionists would support the League in all-India matters, while
the League would abstain from interfering in Punjab politics.
The Unionist leader, Sir Sikander Hyat Khan, even encouraged
his political followers to join also the League, but this
was only to show his goodwill; in Punjab politics the Unionist Party remained firmly in control.

One section of the Muslim landlords in the Punjab were
the religious leaders of the Sufi order, known as *pirs*. The
pir was not necessarily a saint himself; often he had only
inherited the reputation of sainthood from one or more of
his forefathers. He was the guardian of a local shrine to
which the people came for worship and spiritual guidance.
Practically every Muslim family in the Punjab were *murids*
(pupils, followers) of a *pir*, and the *pirs* were therefore
able to wield great influence in local politics. In the
course of time the shrines had come to own much land, presented to them by pious Muslims or granted to them by the
Government in return for political support. The *pirs* therefore had common interests with the ordinary landlords and as
a rule supported the Unionist Party.

During the Second World War the political alignment of
the Punjab changed completely. The Unionist Party wholeheartedly supported the war effort from the beginning and
encouraged Punjabis to join the army. Punjab had traditionally been the major recruiting ground of the Indian army,
and there was no lack of recruits during the first years of

the war. But as early as 1942 the number of recruits di-
minished significantly, and as the Government continued to
request a certain quota from each district, government officials had to employ harsh methods to fulfil the demand.
This soon created a measure of disaffection in the countryside, directed at the Unionist Party.

The disaffection became even worse when in 1943 the Central Government ordered the Punjab Government to requisition
of food-grains. In the Punjab there had been a tendency to
hold back food-grains in order to obtain higher prices so as
to offset the rising prices of other consumer articles; a
member of the Punjab Government had even urged the farmers
to do so. The British Governor of the Punjab warned the
Central Government of the likely political consequences of
the requisition policy, but they were under strong pressure,
both from the Home Government which needed resources for the
war, and from the necessity of procuring food-grains for
Bengal where a severe famine had set in. Furthermore, the
Central Government found it necessary to introduce price
controls, a measure which hit the farming community whose
living standard depended on its ability to obtain a good
price in the market for its main produce, food-grains. These
government measures caused riots in several parts of the province. As the war continued further economic troubles arose
and many ordinary consumer goods became in short supply.
With its firm commitment to the policy of supporting the war,
which caused it all, the Unionist ministry became the target of the disaffection of the farming community.

This situation was exploited by the Muslim League. In
the scheme for a Pakistan which was outlined in the Pakistan
Resolution, the Punjab was the key province; without it the
whole Pakistan idea was meaningless. The League's hands
were tied in some measure by the pact with the Unionists,
but in 1944 a split occurred in the Unionist Party; about
one third of its Assembly members defected and joined the
League. This in effect signalled the death of the pact. The
League had originally attempted to win over the villagers

directly but with little success; the League agitators were
men of the cities who spoke Urdu rather than Punjabi, and
their quotations from the Quran were largely wasted on the
illiterate villagers whose religious point of reference was
the *pir* and his guidance. It was only when the landlords
and the *pirs* became increasingly alienated from the Unionist
Party that the League agitation began to succeed. Here the
existence of close family networks helped to increase the
effect of League agitation: when one man decided to go over
to the League, his relatives tended to follow, as was also
the case when the Assembly members defected in 1944. In
this tactic of appealing to the local notables the *pirs* were
especially important. They understood the Islamic rhetoric
of the League, and they generally had so great an influence
that once won over they could practically guarantee that
those of their *murids* who had the right to vote would follow
suit. Thus it was not the masses that became Muslim Leaguers,
but rather the local magnates, in particular the *pirs*, who
on account of their social status were able to change political allegiance not only for themselves but also, so to
speak, on behalf of their followers.

It should be noted that there was one further reason
for this political shift. The *pirs* and the landlords had
been political allies of the British, and towards the end of
the Second World War they gradually realized, as did every-
one in India, that British rule would soon end. The fear of
coming under the rule of the Congress, the declared policy
of which was one of peasant emancipation and therefore contrary to the interests of great landowners, gave substance
to the League's demand for Pakistan. The League took care
to ensure the landowners that the only way to safeguard their
interests was to make sure that the British Raj was not replaced by a *"Hindu Raj"*, i.e., to support the demand for
Pakistan. This agitation bore handsome fruit: in the provincial election in early 1946 the Muslim League won 75 out
of 86 seats reserved for the Muslims in the Punjab.[3]

Although the North-West Frontier Province was socially

and economically very similar to the Punjab, the political
development there was very different. Until 1932 this province was governed by a Chief Commissioner directly responsible to the Central Government in Delhi, and there was no
popular participation in the provincial government. In the
1920's there arose a social movement for the betterment of
social conditions among the Afghans, i.e., the Pathans, the
dominant ethnic group in the province. In 1929 this movement was reorganised in the Afghan Youth League under the
leadership of Khan Abdul Ghaffar Khan, a medium landowner
from the Peshawar District. Ghaffar Khan was a member of the
Congress from 1928, and during the civil disobedience movement in 1930-32, in which the new organisation became involved, he aligned the Youth League with the Congress. As an
adjunct to the Youth League he organised a corps of volunteers on the Congress model and called them *"Khudai
Khidmatgaran"* or "Servants of God". They were committed to
the Gandhian creed of non-violence and largely succeeded in
keeping their commitment, a fact which was a wonder to the
British and to all India since the Pathans had a reputation
of being inclined towards violence. Ghaffar Khan and his
lieutenants had also approached the Muslim League with a
view to establishing a political alliance, but the League
had decided not to join in the civil disobedience movement
which the Khudai Khidmatgars were eager to do; furthermore
the League at that time represented mainly the Urdu-speaking
Muslims of Hindustan, and for certain historical reasons
they did not get on well with the Pathans. At any rate the
attempt came to nothing, and the Khudai Khidmatgars threw
their lot with the Congress and joined wholeheartedly in the
civil disobedience movement. After the Act of 1935 the
Khudai Khidmatgars organised a provincial political party
known as the Frontier Congress and fought the election in
1937, becoming the largest group in the Frontier Legislative
Assembly but not gaining a majority. After a few months
they were able to form a government, and they ruled the Frontier Province until all Congress provincial governments re-

signed after outbreak of the Second World War.

In the 1937 election the Muslim League had not been
able to put up any candidates for the Frontier Assembly, but
shortly after that it began in earnest to campaign in the
Frontier Province. In the atmosphere which prevailed in India in the period of Congress provincial governments the
League soon succeeded in establishing a Frontier branch
which put up candidates for the following by-elections of
which they won some; in 1939, when the Congress government
resigned there were fourteen Muslim League members in the
Assembly. Their policy consisted in little else than a defence of the interests of the landlords, which were being
attacked by the Congress government. After the Congress re-
signation the League, led by Aurangzeb Khan, made an attempt
to form a new government but failed. The Governor then had
to proclaim governor's rule in accordance with the 1935 constitution. Only in 1943, when the Congress was made practically powerless by British action in retaliation for Gandhi's
"Quit India" campaign, did the League succeed in forming a
government. Lacking a firm party organisation and a coherent
policy Aurangzeb Khan was only able to stay in power by keeping a number of Congress Assembly members in jail.

Towards the end of the war the British began to release
those Congress-men who had been detained, and as soon as the
Congress had regained its strength, the League ministry fell.
The Congress under the leadership of Dr. Khan Sahib, the
brother of Abdul Ghaffar Khan, took office in March 1945 after having promised the British governor to give up civil
disobedience and to support the war effort. The Muslim
League government had not been able to turn the political
development in its favour, such as had been the case in the
Punjab and in Bengal. For the election in early 1946 the
League campaigned only on the Pakistan demand, while the Congress, which had the advantage of a strong party organisation, concentrated on social and economic questions. Out of
the fifty seats in the Assembly the Congress won thirty
(in 1937 they had won nineteen) and the League seventeen.

In view of the Muslim League's electoral successes among the
Muslims everywhere in India, this Congress victory in an almost purely Muslim province was remarkable.[4]

Even with the setback in the North-West Frontier Province Jinnah was now in a strong bargaining position, and he
was determined to exploit it to gain concessions for the Muslims. When the Labour Government in March 1946 - just after
the Indian elections - sent a Cabinet Mission to India to try
to find a formula for the transfer of power to Indian hands,
Jinnah demanded a Pakistan consisting of the six provinces
of the Punjab, The North-West Frontier Province, Sind, Baluchistan, Bengal and Assam. The Congress rejected this demand
outright, and the Cabinet Mission in an attempt to square the
circle then worked out a scheme for the constitution of independent India, according to which the provinces should be
made to form three groups: one consisting of the Muslim provinces in the north-west, one consisting of the Hindu provinces of North, Central and South India and one consisting
of Bengal and Assam. Each group should form its own constitution, and they should be joined together in a union under
a central government with control of only defence, foreign
policy and communications. This scheme was accepted by both
the Congress and the League, although with some misgivings,
in Juni 1946. Then in July Jawaharlal Nehru publicly declared that the Cabinet Mission scheme would probably never
be able to function, since the Congress provinces of the
North-West Frontier and Assam would never accept the grouping,
and that the Central Government must necessarily have more
power than envisaged in order to function at all. Nehru was
probably right, but Jinnah and the League interpreted his
words to mean that the Congress now went back on the earlier
acceptance of the Cabinet Mission plan. In retaliation
Jinnah declared the 16th of August 1946 a "Direct Action"
day, without however explaining what he meant the action to
be. Serious inter-communal riots followed, resulting in
heavy loss of life, in particular in Calcutta. This was in

fact the beginning of a civil war between the Hindu and Muslim communities which continued to grow in intensity until the autumn of 1947 (Hardy 1972, pp. 247-49; Brecher 1959, pp. 316-18).

In this atmosphere all attempts by the Viceroy, Lord Wavell, to revive the Cabinet Mission plan were doomed. In March 1947 he was replaced by Lord Mountbatten who came out with a mandate to transfer power before June 1948. He soon came to the conclusion that a partition of the country - as demanded by the Muslim League - was the only measure which could break the deadlock. The frightful spectacle of the civil war, which was beyond anything the Congress leaders, in particular Nehru, had thought possible, finally convinced the Congress that partition had to be accepted. But the Muslim League did not get the "big" six-province Pakistan they had originally demanded. The claim that Indian Muslims constituted a nation which must have a homeland naturally led to the counter-claim that no Hindu majority area should be forced to belong to the Muslim homeland. Therefore Assam went to India and the two great provinces of Bengal and the Punjab were partitioned so that the Hindu districts went to India and the Muslim districts to Pakistan. The North-West Frontier Province presented a special problem. It was a Muslim majority province and therefore according to the Muslim League had to join Pakistan, but it had a Congress government which was absolutely unwilling to accept partition at all. The League now mounted a campaign for Pakistan in the province and managed to give the impression that a significant proportion of the population were coming over to their side. When the All-India Congress accepted the partition plan, the Frontier Congress felt betrayed and developed vague plans for an autonomous Pakhtunistan. To solve the problem the All-India parties agreed on a referendum which however was boycotted by the Frontier Congress. As a result only fifty-one per cent of the electorate turned out, but of these the vast majority voted for Pakistan, altogether just over fifty per cent of the electorate (Jansson 1981,pp.221-22). The

swing from the Congress to the Muslim League between the
election in early 1946 and the referendum in the summer of
1947 was thus considerable but by no means overwhelming; an
important cause of this swing was the realization by many
people on the Frontier that, given the acceptance of partition by the All-India Congress, any other result would have
placed the province in an impossible situation, since it was
geographically cut off from those areas which were going to
constitute the independent dominion of India.

The independent dominion of Pakistan came into being on
the 14th of August 1947. It became the country of a Muslim
people, but it was not then an Islamic state in any other
sense. As a dominion it was still part of the British Commonwealth and acknowledged the King of England as its Head
of State. The King was represented in the dominions by a
Governor General who as a rule acted in the dominion in the
same way as the King did in Britain, i.e., as a constitutional Head of State without any direct political power.
Jinnah became the first Governor General of independent
Pakistan, but, making use of the Constitution of 1935, assumed what was in practice the same powers as had the Vice-
roys of British India. This tendency to concentrate political power in the hands of one man was undoubtedly a manifestation of the Islamic principle of unitary government
rather than a result of any dictatorial inclinations on
Jinnah's part. There is no doubt that he intended to revise
the political system his country had inherited from the British and to create a kind of "Islamic democracy". He died
however only a year after independence, a tragic loss to the
new nation, and his successor, the able politician Liaqat
Ali Khan, was assassinated in 1951. The subsequent attempts
to make Pakistan an Islamic State proper have demonstrated
the difficulties of reconciling Islamic principles of government with the legacy of the colonial past.

Notes:

1)   For the political aspect of Islam in general, see
      e.g. W. Montgomery Watt, Islamic Political Thought,
      Edinburgh 1968, in particular pp. 116 ff.

2)   This account on Bengal politics is based on Partha
      Chatterjee, 'Bengal Politics and the Muslim Masses,
      1920-1947', in The Jornal of Commonwealth and Com-
      parative Politics, Vol. XX, No. 1 (March 1982), pp.
      25-41.

3)   This account of Punjab politics is based on I.A.
      Talbot, 'The Growth of the Muslims League in the
      Punjab, 1937-1946', in The Journal of Commonwealth
      and Comparative Politics, Vol. XX, No. 1 (March 1982),
      pp. 5-24.

4)   This account of North-West Frontier Province politics
      is based on own studies in National Archives of India,
      New Delhi and in India Office Library, London; and
      on Erland Jansson India, Pakistan or Pakhtunistan?
      The Nationalist Movements in the North-West Frontier
      Province, 1937-47, Uppsala 1981, chapters 5 & 6.
      Detailed references impracticable.

References:

Ahmad, A.   : Islamic Modernism in India and Pakistan
1967   1857-1964. London 1967.

Azad, M.A.K.   : India Wins Freedom.   Bombay 1959.
1959

Brecher, M.   : Nehru.   A Political Biography.   London
1959   1959.

Buckler, F.W.   : "The Political Theory of the Indian
1966   Mutiny". In: Ainslie T. Embree: 1857
                            in India. Mutiny or War of Independence.
                            Boston 1966.

Chatterjee, P.   : "Bengal Politics and the Muslim Masses,
1982   1920-1947". In: The Journal of Common-
                            wealth and Comparative Politics. Vol. XX,
                            No. 1 (March 1982).

Edib, H.   : Inside India.   London 1937.
1937

Hardy, P.   : The Muslims of British India.
1972   Cambridge 1972.

Hunter, W.W.   : The Indian Musalmans.   Reprint Varanasi
1871   1969.

Jansson, E.   : India, Pakistan or Pakhtunistan?   The
1981   Nationalist Movements in the North-West
                            Frontier Province, 1937-47. Uppsala 1981.

Keith, A.B.   : A Constitutional History of India 1600-
1926   1935.   Reprint New York and London 1969.

Mujeeb, M.   : The Indian Muslims.   London 1967.
1967

Naim, C.M. (ed.)   : Iqbal, Jinnah and Pakistan.   Syracuse,
1979   N.Y. 1979.

Nizami, K.A. (ed.)   : Political Letters of Shah Waliullah.
1951   Aligarh 1951, p. 106; quoted in Khalid
                            bin Sayeed: Pakistan. The Formative
                            Phase, 1857-1948. London 1968.

Parry, J.H.   : Europe and a Wider World 1415-1715.
1966   London 1966.

Rizvi, S.A.A.
1977

: Islamic Proselytisation (Seventh to
Sixteenth Centuries)". In: G.A. Oddie
(ed.): Religion in South Asia. New
Delhi 1977.

Russell, R. and
Islam, K.
1969

: Ghalib 1797-1869. Vol. 1. Life and
Letters. London 1969.

bin Sayeed, K.
1968

: Pakistan. The Formative Phase, 1957-
1948. London 1968.

Singhal, D.P.
1972

: Pakistan. Englewood Cliffs, N.J., 1972.

Smith, V.A.
1958

: The Oxford History of India. Rev. ed.
Oxford 1958.

Talbot, I.A.
1982

: "The Growth of the Muslims League in
the Punjab, 1937-1946". In: The Journal
of Commonwealth and Comparative Politics,
Vol. XX, No. 1 (March 1982).

Titus, M.T.
1930

: Islam in India and Pakistan. Madras 1959.

Watt, M.W.
1968

: Islamic Political Thought. Edinburgh
1968.

uz-Zaman, W.
1975

: "Shah Waliullah and His Impact on the
Muslim Freedom Movement". In: A.H. Dani
(ed.): Proceedings of the First Congress
of Pakistan History and Culture.
Islamabad 1975.

Previously published by the
Danish Research Council for the Humanities:

Initiativområdet Islam i Nutiden (Contemporary Islam), Publication no. 1: Islam, Familie og Samfund. Rapport fra Statens Humanistiske Forskningsråds konference på Sandbjerg Slot, 5. - 7. december 1983. Published 1984.

Initiativområdet Islam i Nutiden (Contemporary Islam), Publication no. 2: Litteraturoversigt: Islam, Familie og Samfund. Ved Søren Skou Rasmussen. Published 1984.

By Aarhus University Press and the
Jutland Archaeological Society:

Atlas of the Stone Age Cultures of Qatar. By Holger Kapel. 96 pages, illustrated. 1968.

Preliminary Survey in East Arabia. By T.G. Bibby. 67 pages, illustrated, hardbound. 1973.

Nuristani Buildings. By Lennart Edelberg. 223 pages, illustrated, hardbound. 1984.